Power Over Rationality

SUNY Series in the Making of Foreign Policy: Theories and Issues
Alex Roberto Hybel, Editor

Power Over Rationality

The Bush Administration and the Gulf Crisis

Alex Roberto Hybel

State University of New York Press

Published by
State University of New York Press

© 1993 State University of New York

For information, address State University of New York
Press, State University Plaza, Albany, N.Y. 12246

Production by E. Moore
Marketing by Lynne Lekakis

Library of Congress Cataloging-in-Publication Data

Hybel, Alex Roberto.
  Power over rationality: the Bush administration and the Gulf
crisis / Alex Roberto Hybel.
    p. cm. — (SUNY series in the making of foreign policy)
  Includes bibliographical references and index.
  ISBN 0-7914-1421-3 (acid-free paper). — ISBN 0-7914-1422-1
(Pbk.: acid-free paper)
    1. Persian Gulf War, 1991—United States—Decision-making.
2. United States—Foreign relations—1989- —Decision-making.
3. Bush, George, 1924- —Views on the Persian Gulf War. 4. Bush,
George, 1924- —Knowledge—Persian Gulf Region. I. Title.
II. Series.
DS79.724.U6H9   1993
973.928—dc20
                                                      92-10663
                                                      CIP

10 9 8 7 6 5 4 3 2

To my wife Jan and our daughters
Sabrina Alexandra and Gabriela Marissa

Contents

Foreword

This is a provocative book, not just because it advances a critical theory or a counter-intuitive interpretation but also because it poses important and tough questions about some crucial issues of both social science inquiry and contemporary U.S. foreign policy. Such is Alex Roberto Hybel's purpose: to stir thought about how one teases meaning out of the welter of phenomena relevant to the conduct of world affairs in general and the United States in particular. Readers are offered repeated opportunities to ponder alternative explanations even as Professor Hybel suggests a way of constructively synthesizing them. As a result, he provides readers with the power to fit the pieces of foreign policy puzzles together on their own and a host of good reasons why they are well-advised to exercise this power on behalf of greater comprehension.

The tough questions posed here revolve around the issue of rationality in world affairs. Although he does not say it in so many words, Hybel rightly presumes that adherence to the tenets of rational behavior can, other things being equal, have beneficial consequences for both those who act in the public arena and those toward whom the actions are directed. But, as he emphasizes, others things are rarely equal. A wide array of dynamics can intrude at a number of points in the processes through which foreign policy decisions are made and actions subsequently taken. The intrusions can originate with demands in the external world, with stresses and strains of the domestic scene, with rivalries that sustain governmental bureaucracies, and with distortions in the minds and hearts of officials. So pervasive and inevitable are the intrusions, in fact, that pure rationality—the kind in which action flows from a thorough assessment of the alternative means to move toward clearly specified goals on the basis of full and accurate information and frequent post-decision feedback—is beyond realization. Time is too scarce, information is too imperfect, resources are too limited, people are too flawed, and organizations are too cumbersome for rationality to ever carry the day in the policy-making process. The most that can be accomplished is a minimization of the obstacles to rational action, a continuous attention to the possibility of distortion, an ever-present readiness to correct for the mistakes that take policies off course.

Endless questions flow from an awareness that policy is destined to be less than rational: Do the prevailing conditions of world politics determine policy outcomes irrespective of the calculations and resolve of policy makers? Are the international and domestic forces which play upon officials so powerful and pervasive as to dictate their choices irrespective of their values and talents? Does it matter, that is, who the officials are, what their experiences have been, or how ambitious they may be? Dare one argue that causation is exclusively located in the perceptions and misperceptions of the individuals who decide on a course of action? Is it possible to synthesize the various sources of foreign policy in such a way as to allow for an interplay between the objective forces of world politics and the subjective interpretation of them by policy makers? If the latter know they are susceptible to misperception—to a need to maintain cognitive balances, group harmonies, and hierarchical arrangements at the expense of an accurate grasp of the situations they seek to affect—can they not offset their vulnerabilities and thereby ensure effective and efficient policy choices?

The answers to such questions are not self-evident. They can be varied as the theories one employs to attribute causal strength to the diverse factors at work in a situation. And to the extent situations are marked by unique demands, then to that extent will note also have to be taken of varying answers to the foregoing questions. There is, in other words, an interaction between the observers and their theories on the one hand and the actors and their situational circumstances on the other. If the actors conduct themselves in ways not anticipated by the theories of the observers, then explanation and understanding are bound to be faulty. It follows that cogent foreign policy analysis requires both sound theory and incisive empirical description that sorts out the relevant from the irrelevant, differentiates between causes and effects, allows for the intensity of motives, anticipates the likelihood of misperception, or otherwise accounts for deviations from the rational path.

It is the strength of this book that Professor Hybel offers both the theoretical and empirical materials out of which keen understanding is developed. His empirical focus is the Bush administration's policies designed to meet and reverse Iraq's conquest of Kuwait in 1990; but to the details of this case he brings a number of theoretical perspectives, noting their strengths and weaknesses in the light of the evolving circumstances of the Gulf War. Here readers can witness the interplay of actors and their goals, states and their constraints, decision-making organizations and their rivalries, individuals and their reasoning, all juxtaposed in the context of rational deterrence theory, attribution theory, cognitive consistency theory, and schema theory. Doubtless time will yield diplomatic and policy-making documents that necessitate alterations in Professor Hybel's early account of decision-making high in the Bush administration, but the virtues of his analysis will not be undermined by subsequent modifications of the empirical materials. On the contrary, any new facts that emerge can be readily accommodated by the theoretical constructs he provides.

In short, this is more than another case study. Its enduring contribution is that it provides the context within which any case materials relevant to the conduct of foreign policy can be evaluated. So let the reader enjoy this brief tour of two horizons, one that depicts a crucial moment in international history and another that brings that moment vividly alive with insight and meaning.

James N. Rosenau

Preface

It has been traditionally assumed that men and women make history. Few have captured this idea better than Thucydides some twenty-five centuries ago. Conscious that city-states were restrained by international necessities, he observed that it was up to their leaders to design policies that widened the range of choice.[1] But he also noted that different leaders were not impelled by the same passions, beliefs, or intentions, and did not possess the same leadership qualities. In Pericles, Thucydides found a ruler who rekindled the Athenian spirit and recognized the obstacles Athens had to surmount in order to sustain choice. In Cleon, he encountered a ruler who used violence to promote not Athens's well-being but his own—a man who possessed "a vulgar mind, acute in a second-rate manner, without intelligence or humanity."[2] It was on Pericles' shoulders that Thucydides placed Athens's hope, but it was Cleon's selfishness and meanness that helped bring about its downfall.

The interest expressed by Thucydides regarding the role leaders play as they seek to promote their states' objectives remained intact through the centuries. But then came Marx, and said to the world: "The mode of production of material life conditions the social, political, and intellectual life process in general. It is not the consciousness of men that determines their being, but on the contrary, their social being that determines their consciousness."[3] Marx did not intend to argue that men and women did not have choices and could not alter their social environment.[4] His words, however, weighed heavily on the minds of subsequent generations.

Influenced by the fear that the individual was being dehumanized by uncaring systems, and by the conviction that they could help alter such systems, social scientists began to probe their nature. Early successes inspired them to search deeper for better answers. In time, however, they lost sight of the fact that their original intent was to free the individual, not to forget him. Their remissness made the individual less relevant—an entity too weak to combat society's forces.

Scientific research without shared paradigms is impossible.[5] But adherence to a set of paradigms also has the tendency to bind its promoters to a very narrow perspective of what is acceptable. The belief that structures mattered more than the thoughts and actions of individuals developed long and rigid tentacles, that extended into all but a few social science fields. In international politics, students lost interest on how foreign policy makers reasoned and why they reasoned the way they did. They accounted for the decisions and actions of foreign policy makers as part of rational processes responding to objective obstacles and opportunities. Foreign policy makers stopped being men and women with unique identities and became actors whose roles were defined entirely by situations, power, and interests.

To focus on decision makers is not deny the existence of systemic forces, but to view them through the eyes of those who must respond to their presence. This strategy is costly. Its most immediate victims are accuracy and parsimony. Data depicting the beliefs, values, and intentions of decision makers are difficult to access and unreliable. Moreover, cognitive models are inherently more complex than those that rely solely on power, national interest, and rationality. But if our ultimate goal is to understand better the nature of international politics, these obstacles should not deter us.

This book and the series in which it is presented, "The Making of Foreign Policy: Theories and Issues," are modest attempts to help revive the idea that decision makers matter. For some, the empirical content of the book may seem questionable. Some may wonder whether it is wise to address the nature of the decision-making process during the Gulf crisis by relying on so few empirical sources, published not long after the event itself had ended.

I think it is. Undoubtedly, as memoirs by members of the Bush administration are published and new documents released, many of the conclusions arrived here will come under attack. But such a risk comes with the territory.[6] The intent of this book is not to put forward the last word on what transpired at the White House, Department of State, and Department of Defense. Instead, its objective is to propose a typology of decision-making aptitudes designed to explain foreign policy decisions and to assess the quality of the process. The handling of the Gulf crisis by the Bush administration is presented primarily as an example to demonstrate the typology's theoretical and practical value.

My indebtedness to others for the content of this book is substantial. Students come and go, and after a while most of them become part of a blur in our memory. But students at the School of International Relations at the University of Southern California were the ones who, as I voiced some of the theoretical ideas I have managed finally to put on paper, provoked me to rethink them, be clearer, and more precise. I also benefited extensively from the comments I received from Robert Keohane, Dwain Mefford, and anonymous reviewers. In addition, I am forever thankful to Thomas Biersteker, Stephen Lamy, Abraham Lowenthal, John Odell, James Rosenau, and Ronald Steel. Although they never read this manuscript as it was being put together, their friendship and unbending support made its completion possible. As always, I am very grateful to my mother-in-law, Barbara Peurifoy, for editing the final draft. And finally, I must extend my appreciation to Connecticut College for providing the funds necessary to complete the project.

Chapter One

Power, War, and Decision-Making Aptitudes

The very powerful can afford not to be rational. Inordinate amounts of power free decision makers from having to engage in systematic-decision making procedures to attain their objectives. Even amongst the powerful, however, success without rationality is not eternal. The presence of rationality in an uncertain world cannot guarantee victory, but its repeated absence courts disaster.

To many Americans, the Gulf War symbolized the end of the Vietnam syndrome and the beginning of a new era. A war that many experts claimed would drag on for months, result in the deaths of thousands of young American soldiers, and split the nation into rancorous factions, brought about precisely the opposite effects. Forty-eight days after the war had begun, and at the cost of but 146 American lives, the United States succeeded in preserving its access and that of the industrialized world to the Arabian oil fields.[1]

The victory might tempt some to assume that the outcome had to be the culmination of a well-thought-out, highly sophisticated decision-making process within the Bush administration. This book challenges such an assumption not by uncovering new facts, but by focusing with a critical eye on how problems were defined, goals identified, alternatives evaluated, and policies selected. This challenge has as its intellectual root a typology of decision-making aptitudes derived from the propositions posited by three cognitive theories—attribution, schema, and cognitive consistency—and comes in the form of two interrelated arguments. The first argument, which is entirely theoretical, sets the framework for the second argument, which is theoretical, empirical, and normative.

Attempts to infuse explanations of U.S. foreign policy making with a theoretical perspective have been dominated by the assumption that decision makers act rationally.[2] Convinced that to "search for the clue to foreign policy exclusively in the motives of statesmen is both futile and deceptive," Hans Morgenthau sought to persuade American scholars of the 1940s that the most effective way to give form to the relationship between a state's national interest and power was through rationality.[3] Encumbered by the conviction that the Second World War would have been averted had the United States and France used their power earlier to bloc Germany's hegemonic aspiration, and by the need to answer to the new challenges brought into the international environment by the Soviet Union's emergence as a superpower, U.S. scholars and foreign policy practitioners embraced Morgenthau's logic. His model, they concluded, was theoretically sound and would help promote the interests and gratify the appetites of the United States.

A less-than-wise idea became theory and then dogma. As time went by, the advocates of Realism and rationalism lost sight of the fact that Morgenthau's theoretical perspective had little to say about the "real" world of foreign policy making.[4] They did not keep in mind that Morgenthau, conscious that foreign policies had rarely been the result of rational processes, had created a model designed not to explain and predict, but to dictate, how leaders *ought* to reason.[5]

In time, some scholars began to challenge this heavy reliance on rationality. They accepted Morgenthau's dictum that only a "rational policy minimizes risks and maximizes benefits."[6] But they also emphasized that if a rational foreign policy was the ultimate goal, it was imperative to uncover the obstacles in the cognition of humans that might impede its attainment. With this mission in mind, these scholars attempted to give meaning to the large number of elements that undermine the ability of decision makers to reach past their cognitive confines. Through their work we finally began to understand why the Truman administration, after having voiced little concern about South Korea's fate, rushed to its aid and became entangled in a war that would result in a stalemate; why the Kennedy administration, although led by "the best and the brightest," handled the Castro regime as only an unskilled novice would; or why the Johnson and Nixon administrations lost South Vietnam to a nation much weaker than the United States and plunged America into its worst international nightmare.[7]

Four scholars stood above the crowd. Alexander L. George, by reviving and refining Nathan Leites' "operational code," further reinforced the long-standing belief that the tactics and strategies relied on by foreign policy makers to address international problems are in part a function of their beliefs. A few years later, by merging cybernetics with cognitive consistency theory, John Steinbruner demonstrated why foreign policy makers so rarely adhere to the rules of rationality and why they seldom seek solutions that wander far from past courses of action or that offset their cognitive balance. Steinbruner's work was soon followed by Robert Axelrod's heroic attempt to recreate the cognitive maps used by foreign policy makers to "derive explanations of the past, make predictions for the future, and choose policies in the present." And then came Robert Jervis. His book *Perception and Misperception*, first published in 1976, was not original in content. Its beauty and strength lay in providing an intellectual synthesis of psychological theories and findings and their applicability to foreign policy making.[8]

Although admired for their intent, these studies did not generate wide support. Their nature demanded data rarely available, and when attainable, often unreliable. Moreover, these works seldom attempted to place in a coherent framework the different "variables" that could intercede in the decision-making process. A broad range of psychological and sociological factors were believed to affect the way humans made decisions, but nobody knew how to gauge their significance or how to apply them as multiple "causal" variables. These problems were compounded by the fact that the applied psychological and sociological factors were borrowed from theories generated in fields permeated by dissonance.

Today, the study of foreign policy making stands at a crossroads. New works by Deborah Larson, Dwain Mefford, Philip Schrodt, and myself, to name just a few, are applying the latest works in artificial intelligence, linguistics, and cognitive psychology in order to design formal models of foreign policy making and to provide the field with a sounder theoretical foundation.[9] The obstacles faced by my colleagues and I are somewhat less formidable than those encountered by our intellectual ancestors. Vast improvements in computer technology and greater access to more detailed information about the cognitive nature of decision makers may help enhance the relevance of these studies.

Overall, however, students of international politics continue to be enamored with structures and how they impact on the relationships between states. Those who share this affection pay little attention to the roles of decision makers; and when they do, almost invariably they attach the adjective "rational." The latest changes in the international environment have not tarnished their enchantment. As they seek to understand how the international system will be affected by the dissolution of the Soviet Union; by the attempt by Eastern European countries to redefine themselves as political, economic, and social entities; and by the struggle by Middle Eastern states to give form to a new regional structure—these analysts are inclined to disregard the roles played by those who pushed for these changes, or else to perceive them as mere abstract, rational entities, differentiated only by the interests they promote. For the most part, they continue to assume that the actions of such leaders were a function of the structural forces faced by their states.

Structural constraints do impose themselves on states, but decision makers do not always respond to them in the same manner. Their beliefs, values, and intellectual capabilities affect their perceptions of constraints, and determine the types of solutions they try to design.

Contemporary cognitive psychologists inform us that the problem solver can be conceptualized as a seeker of attributable causes, or of analogical schemes, or of cognitive consistency.[10] The first perspective views the decision maker as an untrained scientist interested in finding causal relationships as he struggles to understand the universe and make decisions. If he is not entirely rational, it is because he is ignorant of his own inadequacies and not because of some cognitive need. The second approach perceives the policy maker as an individual burdened by the lack of time and energy, and by a limited intellectual capacity. He compensates for these shortcomings by searching for a generic concept, stored in his memory in the form of a schema, that can be imposed as a solution on the problem at hand. The third method envisions the problem solver as a character living in an uncertain world permeated with conflicting values, and hampered by his need to achieve a tolerable balance between his beliefs, values, and cognition. As he defines problems and selects policies, he attains cognitive consistency by disregarding information that challenge his preconceptions and by ignoring values that conflict with those he is trying to promote.

These three cognitive perspectives share rationality as their reference point. Cognitive consistency, with its assumption that no problem solver has the capacity to overcome fully his cognitive needs, is located the farthest from the ideal process.[11] Schema theory, with its contention that the decision maker attempts to make inferences and judgments with a minimum expenditure of energy, time, and thought, stands at the middle of the decision-making aptitude spectrum. And attribution theory, with its belief that the decision maker acts as a "naive" scientist, is located closest to the rational decision making mode.

These competing perspectives can be used in at least two ways. Until recently, they have been applied concurrently to a variety of cases to gauge their explanatory reach.[12] It is doubtful, however, that any one perspective would be comprehensive enough to explain the decisions of the universe of decision makers, even if such universe were to be very small. Foreign policy makers do not all possess the same intellectual ability to make decisions, and some have a greater need than others to maintain cognitive balance. It is not unreasonable, therefore, to assume that to explain the decision of more than one decision maker we must use more than one theory. If this is the case, then by associating a theory with a particular decision maker it would be feasible to determine that individual's ability to function rationally.

The theoretical and practical significance of any typology is determined by its applicability. To gauge the utility of the typology just proposed lies beyond the scope of this book. A glimpse of its relevance, however, will be given in this book's second section as it addresses two questions:

1. Why did the United States fail to prevent Iraq's invasion of Kuwait?
2. Why did the United States go to war against Iraq?

Deterrence, propose Alexander George and Richard Smoke, entails "the persuasion of one's opponent that the costs and/or risks of a given course of action he might take outweigh its benefits."[13] Theorists of deterrence differentiate between the "failure to conduct a policy of deterrence" and "deterrence failure." Analysis of the first type of failure entails explaining why a group of foreign policy makers did not contemplate deterrence as a viable policy or decided that its implementation was unnecessary. Analysis of deterrence failure entails explaining why a policy of deterrence failed to stop the aggressor from doing what he was warned not to do.

Iraq's invasion of Kuwait signifies for the United States a failure of the first type. The decision not to implement a policy of deterrence can result when the potential aggressor conceals information from his target or deceives him about his intention, rationale, strategy, capability, target, and/or time; or it can result when the potential victim fails to derive the correct estimates although he has the information to do so. Blame for the United States' failure to predict Iraq's invasion of Kuwait must to be placed squarely not on Saddam Hussein or the U.S. intelligence community, but on President George Bush's top advisers.[14] By late July 1990, Saddam Hussein had given the United States ample opportunity to infer his intentions and to deter him if it found them objectionable. The U.S. intelligence community, after monitoring closely the movement of Saddam's military forces in Iraq, informed the Bush administration that an attack on Kuwait was very likely. President Bush's top foreign policy advisers rejected the assessment.

To implement a policy of deterrence, the observer must first be able to question, and alter if necessary, his image of the would-be aggressor. Influenced by their own dependence on analogical reasoning, the central figures within the Bush administration assumed that Saddam would not invade Kuwait because he was a rational actor and had learned from Iraq's war with Iran how costly another major war would be. Brent Scowcroft, Richard Cheney, Colin Powell and Norman Schwarzkopf held fast to this belief even after they had been warned by the Defence Intelligence Agency and Central Intelligence Agency that Iraq was getting ready to attack Kuwait.

Pentagon officials played a critical role in the assessment. They knew that if they accepted the argument that Iraq intended to attack Kuwait, the only way to stop the invasion would be for the United States to threaten to retaliate with its own military power. However, humiliated by the Vietnam war and the fiasco in Lebanon in 1983, the top military leaders were determined not to use force as an instrument of deterrence unless the political leaders defined with the utmost clarity the political and military goals and authorized the usage of whatever means were needed to fulfill them.

The ease with which the United States defeated Iraq has persuaded a large number of analysts that the decision to go to war was rational. This book takes a different stand. It contends that although the effect of a policy is always important, rationality is a function not of effect but of process. Based on this proposition, this book argues that the decision to go to war against Iraq was not the upshot of a process one would hope from the government that rules the most powerful state in the international system.

A rational response to any major problem entails gathering the information necessary to delineate the full nature of the problem, identifying and evaluating the goals and their interrelationships, isolating the pertinent alternatives and estimating their probable consequences, and choosing the alternative with the highest expected utility. George Bush and Brent Scowcroft prevented the "rational" execution of these steps. They alone determined that the United States would: 1) refuse to tolerate Iraq's attempt to impose its will on Kuwait and possibly Saudi Arabia, because such a change in the status quo would give Saddam Hussein extensive control over the oil market; 2) deploy its forces over Saudi territory, if authorized to do so by Saudi leaders, to protect it from a possible Iraqi attack; 3) not wait to see whether containment would succeed in persuading Saddam to pull out of Kuwait; and 4) resort to violence, if necessary, to expel Iraq from Kuwait. All these steps were taken by Bush and Scowcroft with almost no input from Middle Eastern experts, and without eliciting alternative interpretations and possible solutions of the problem from other top foreign policy officials.

Bush and Scowcroft relied on two analogies to design their decisions. From the 1938 Munich debacle they deduced that appeasement never pacifies tyrants. Since Saddam Hussein was another Adolf Hitler, the only choice left to the United States was to act aggressively. This meant two things: 1) protecting Saudi Arabia, and 2) going to war against Iraq, if necessary, in order to free Kuwait. A decision not to protect Saudi Arabia would have been viewed by Saddam as a lack of resolve on the part of the United States and, thus, as an invitation to continue with his policy of expansion. Moreover, a policy of containment would have signaled Saddam that the United States and its allies lacked the will to make hard choices, and that if he stood fast the alliance would eventually falter.

Before deciding that a military operation against Saddam and his military establishment was a viable option, however, Bush and Scowcroft had to cope with another important memory: Vietnam. For the two decision makers, the central lesson to be inferred from that nightmare was that the United States should never get involved in another major conflict unless it was willing to use the military power it needed to win the war swiftly and impressively.

In sum, this book contends that the foreign policy process adopted by Bush and his closest advisers during the Gulf crisis was a function of their dependence on two analogies, and that this dependence was so intense that it undermined their ability to contemplate alternative definitions of the problem and to give serious thought to other policy options. Members of the Bush administration, in other words, relied on historical analogies not only to define and respond to the Gulf crisis, but also to maintain an acceptable level of cognitive balance as they made decisions.

The study of international affairs is usually divided into the analysis of international politics and of foreign policy. Students of international politics focus on macro questions, while students of foreign policy address micro issues. The environments studied by the two groups do not exist independent of one another. As Kenneth Waltz notes, different international structures tend to create different expectations on the part of foreign policy makers.[15] But Waltz and other structuralists assume that rationality is a constant—that it does not vary with changes in a state's location in the structure of the international system. They presume, for instance, that the leaders of an unchallenged hegemonic state are as rational as those who preside over a state losing its hegemony. This study contends that the assumption is unjustified, and proposes that the leaders of a state experience a greater need to be rational when they believe that the state is vulnerable to the actions of other states than when they believe it is not. More specifically, it proposes that the absence of vulnerability frees decision makers from the fear of making mistakes which in turn, free them from the need to think rationally.

Based on the above proposition, this study argues that without the Soviet Union as a veritable counterbalance in the Middle East, the Bush administration had little incentive to view Iraq's invasion of Kuwait rationally. Knowing full well that the United States had the military power to defeat Iraq, the only major step the Bush administration had to take was to permit the Pentagon to use whatever means it needed in order to achieve its assigned objective swiftly and at a relatively low cost.

Having identified the principal impediments to rationality, this study closes with a short discussion of how the proposed typology of decision-making aptitudes can help leaders of democratic states improve the quality of their states' foreign policy-making processes. It does so by bringing into perspective the dilemma faced by the leaders of a powerful democratic state who are determined to define the structure of the international system but need to be responsive to the expectations of a citizenry that, while not particularly competent about international matters, often demands a voice.

Chapter Two

A Typology of Decision-Making Aptitudes

Introduction

Rationality in decision making is a desirable but elusive goal. Its realization, moreover, does not guarantee success. In a world where decisions are made without complete information, leaders sometimes opt for the wrong alternative, regardless of how rational they are. But if rationality is no panacea, it does reduce distinctly the room for error. Rationality facilitates the depiction of a problem's nature, the collection of information, the isolation and ranking of values, the identification of possible alternatives, the calculation of the costs and benefits the implementation of each alternative could elicit, the selection of the best option, and the monitoring of its effectiveness.

Rationality has a lofty tradition in Western civilization. It is rooted in the ideas of Socrates, Aristotle, the Stoics, and

see also page 104

the Epicureans, who proposed that with perfect knowledge humans would do the correct and moral thing and would, as a result, live happier and better lives. Until the seventeenth century it was common to hope that humans could be taught to behave as purposeful, rational creatures. The modern world appropriated this idea and placed it in a narrower context. Adam Smith, in *The Wealth of Nations*, proposed that society would be more efficient if its members acted dispassionately to advance their own self-interest. In the nineteenth century, Jeremy Bentham, determined to counteract challengers who contended that the pursuit of self-interest had helped undermine society's well-being, maintained that rational individuals act with the intent of promoting the general good because it is in their self-interest to avert social recrimination during life and eternal punishment upon death.[1]

The end of the Second World War helped propagate the idea that humans also could be perceived as rational international actors. Convinced that in an anarchical system world actors can rely only on themselves to protect and advance their own interests, foreign policy theorists and analysts proposed that each state be viewed as a unitary rational entity. Decision makers comprising the official, bureaucratic manifestation of a state were assumed to act as a body with a single mind, capable of formulating foreign policies based on rational calculations of the effect such policies would have on the state's power. As noted by Hans Morgenthau, to give meaning to the raw material of foreign policy, i.e., power, political reality must be approached with a rational outline.[2]

This perspective, typically referred to as Realism, has been the target of two types of criticism. One group, claiming that the globe cannot afford many more wars, the continuing economic disparity that separates states, and the indiscriminate consumption of resources that foul the environment at an ever-increasing pace, argues that Realism foments these behaviors. Rationality used for the sole purpose of advancing a state's cause, they note, is seldom used to understand or care for the effects a state's policies has on the overall well-being of the international system.

Order vs Anarchy

Contemporary Realists recognize that in an anarchical system the aforementioned tendencies are difficult to control. But they emphasize also that in the absence of a global government—one that would be nearly impossible to regulate and monitor—Realism helps mitigate the forces of anarchism. Adherence to Realism, they contend, promotes order and sets up the structural conditions that facilitate cooperation between states.

Order, continue some of these analysts, is a necessary condition for the evolution of a more desirable international system, and is made possible when Realism dictates the behavior of powerful states. The structure of the international system is defined by the powers of the powerful. These actors have the means to dictate and enforce the forms of behavior they want. Driven by the commitment to allocate their resources as efficiently as possible, they seek to reduce uncertainty in the international system. Moreover, although the structure of the international system will not serve as well the interests of the less powerful (since it was not designed with their interests in mind), in most cases they will favor its presence. So long as the structure provides them with some room to maneuver, the less powerful rationalize that it is better to function under a system that, although repressive, enables them to identify the obstacles and design their policies accordingly, than under one in which uncertainty is so prevalent that the creation and implementation of any policy becomes routinely a potentially costly gamble.[3] Order, conclude defenders of Realism, will not eliminate all wars, eradicate economic inequalities between states, and elicit full-fledged commitments from its makers to consume only those resources that do not endanger the environment. But its presence is "desirable because it is the condition of the realization of other [international] values."[4]

Until recently, few analysts viewed cooperation between states as Realism's forte. Convinced that in an anarchical system states are constantly at war or preparing for war, Realists of earlier years nurtured the idea that cooperation was rarely advisable. They emphasized that in a zero-sum game a state's only rational and affordable strategy is to enhance constantly its instruments of violence and to remain aloof from any cooperative venture.

Non-Realists deplored this philosophy. They questioned the wisdom of promoting an idea that not only was false— for in their minds international politics was, or could be made to be, a positive-sum game—but also helped increase rather than lessen, existing divisions. A few contemporary Realists took note of these challenges and recognized that their theory could account for cooperation without having to transform radically its nature.

Inspired by the increased interdependence between states and their heightened reluctance to rely on instruments of violence to resolve their differences, a new batch of Realists began to formulate arguments that sought to explain the birth and evolution of regimes in the international system. These regimes, they noted, were created not by selfless actors, but by egoists who realized that on some occasions a positive-sum game is preferable to a zero-sum game. The flourishing of a variety of international regimes made it evident to Realists that a willingness by international actors to acquiesce to the principles, norms, rules, and decision-making procedures of a regime did not signify that such actors were placing the well-being of the group above their own, but that they had concluded that their independent interests would be served better by joining forces with others than by pursuing them independently.[5]

Skeptics wondered whether this new development was a function of the recognition by international actors that at times they must be willing to cooperate with others to attain their goals, or of their recognition that when a hegemon proposes the creation of a regime and invites various parties to become members, it is not in their interest to refuse the invitation. This concern was justified. The study of international regimes showed that their creation was associated almost invariably with the concerns and interests of a particular hegemon.

The manner in which most regimes came into being posed a major challenge to those who had argued that cooperation was not anomalous in an anarchical world. Although it was acknowledged that regimes intended to benefit all of its members, not just the hegemon, and that an institution would not be identified as a regime if any of its members had been coerced to join, it was unclear whether a regime would be able to endure the withering of its principal actor. This challenge was taken up by Robert Keohane.

In a book that seeks to be both theoretical and normative, Keohane reaffirms the earlier belief that egoists are rational enough to comprehend that cooperation does not signify sacrificing one's interests for those of others. Cooperation, maintains Keohane, is the by-product of various rational processes in which competing parties, seeking to promote their independent selfish interests, conclude that their separate causes can be served by joining forces and agreeing to adhere to a particular standard of behavior. A regime, he adds, not only exposes its members to the benefits of cooperation, but also teaches them the art of cooperation. Thus, when the regime's hegemon begins to lose its power, its members need not relinquish their membership automatically. If each concludes that by maintaining its association it will be better off than by traveling on an independent path, its independent choices will be to try to keep the regime in place, possibly with a slightly modified structure.[6]

In sum, although Realists originally argued that rationality must be practiced by international actors for the purpose of protecting and promoting their states' national interests and that such practice entailed constantly preparing for war, some are now suggesting that rationality in Realism also can contribute to greater stability and cooperation. But do actors really act rationally in the pursuit of their states' national interests? This is the second challenge posed to Realism.

In the late 1960s and throughout the larger part of the 1970s, the study of foreign policy experienced a critical metamorphosis. Convinced that the "mind of man, for all its marvels, is a limited instrument," various scholars began to view the premises of rationalism as unrealistic and to posit powerful arguments for analyzing foreign policy not from the perspective of an objective reality ready to be grasped in its true context by decision makers, but from the perspective of the decision makers' cognitions. Studies by Alexander George, John Steinbruner, Robert Axelrod, and Robert Jervis brought new excitement to the field. Their work helped move the study of foreign policy making away from the "ideal" world of decision making into a more "real" environment.

The initial exhilaration, however, was soon replaced by doubt and frustration. Attempts to carry out sophisticated empirical analyses were hindered by the existence of competing psychological theories, the unavailability of reliable data, and the presence of ambiguous concepts and unquantifiable variables. All this was compounded by the tendency to develop explanations that were less parsimonious than those posited by orthodox theories.[7]

For a while it seemed that Realism would once again dominate the field. Parsimony and an emphasis on rationality returned to center court, while studies that focused on the cognitive processes of foreign policy makers were relegated to the sidelines.[8] But finally, in 1985, Deborah Larson made a valiant attempt to demonstrate the value of understanding the types of cognitive processes foreign policy makers engage in as they cope with international problems.[9]

In earlier studies, students of foreign policy making tended to borrow psychological concepts from various cognitive theories. This tendency made it extremely difficult to explain the nature of the decision-making process and to formulate a theory of foreign policy making.[10] Larson sought to change this approach by proposing that it would be more rewarding to compare the explanatory value of alternative psychological theories. As she notes, the application of different theories can help uncover important explanatory variables and possible relationships that might be overlooked were one to cling to the old ways of incorporating cognitive variables.[11]

Larson's suggestion is intellectually appealing. Since social psychologists are a long way from resolving their theoretical differences, students of foreign policy must continue to test competing cognitive approaches. But an important caveat must be introduced at this point. Each cognitive theory is designed to explain the cognitive processes of *all* its subjects. For the analyst of U.S. foreign policy making, this means testing the explanatory reach of competing cognitive theories by focusing on the reasoning processes of very different U.S. foreign policy makers, e.g., leaders as different as Dwight Eisenhower and Ronald Reagan. To the reader who has a general understanding of how these two individuals approached international problems, this suggestion will seem absurd. Although at times Eisenhower might have rationalized international problems in terms of simple categories and might have used analogies, his analytical capabilities were far superior to those of Reagan.[12]

Based on the argument and example just presented, skeptics are likely to challenge this study's interpretation of rationality. Thus, before continuing, it is important to air some of these challenges and respond to them.

According to Christopher Achen and Duncan Snidal, critics of rational models often commit the "descriptivist fallacy." It is their contention that any person who has read the appropriate texts will immediately recognize that the axioms and utility theory typically presented in any rational theory "refer only to choices. Mental calculations are never mentioned: the theory makes no reference to them." A rational theory, they conclude, "is agnostic about the actual calculations decision makers undertake."[13]

Achen and Snidal are wrong on two counts. First, they are wrong when they contend that rational deterrence theory refers only to what Frank Zagare defines as "instrumental rationality." As Zagare notes, the concept of rationality can be either procedural or instrumental. Procedural rationality, which has been articulated by scholars as diverse as Herbert Simon, Sidney Verba, and Graham Allison, focuses on the actual decision-making process. A rational decision maker is one who, when confronted with a problem that requires a solution, gathers information, ranks his values, delineates and assesses a wide range of alternatives, and makes a choice guided by his want to maximize his returns. Instrumental rationality, on the other hand, refers to nothing more than an individual's ability to impose connected and transitive preferences over a set of available outcomes; such an individual, when confronted with two or more alternatives which give rise to different outcomes, will select the one which yields his preferred outcome.[14] At the outset, thus, it is inappropriate for Achen and Snidal to contend that critics of rational deterrence theory have committed the "descriptivist fallacy." The most that they can argue, at this juncture, is that their critics' interpretations of rationality differ from their own, and that it is unreasonable to rely on one standard to evaluate a theory which depends on a different standard.

Second, Achen and Snidal are wrong in their contention that utility theory refers to choices, not to mental calculations. As they note, a rational actor is one who, in view of his exogenously given preferences and options, will try to optimize his preferences in light of other actors' preferences and options. Let us fully accept this definition and ask: Can the actor in question "optimize his preferences in light of other actors' preferences and options" without engaging in a "rational mental calculation" if the situation requires that he estimate its *expected value*? In complex situations, he cannot. A decision maker who faces outcomes with different payoffs, and who has options with different probabilities for attaining what he seeks, cannot engage in a rational choice without first conducting rational mental calculations.[15] Moreover, by accepting Anatol Rapoport's contention that it is from a decision maker's choice that the theoretician constructs his utility scale in which all the outcomes are assigned numbers, rather than from the *a priori* identification of his preferences and the probability values he assigned to his different options (regardless of how difficult both tasks may be), Achen and Snidal are literally promoting the idea that it is acceptable to formulate tautological arguments. No wonder arguments advanced by those who resort to rational deterrence theory are nearly impossible to falsify.[16]

Achen, Snidal, and many other defenders of rationality seem to have forgotten that rationality, was originally promoted as an ideal. Ideals, as generally understood, can be sought but rarely attained. By imposing on reality an ideal, the analyst creates an "unreal" reality. Foreign policy is about acts initiated not by unreal, abstract individuals, but by men and women with strong interests and beliefs, different attitudes about how problems should be addressed, and diverse decision-making capabilities.

Ideals, however, do have purposes. The ideal of rationality can be used as a standard, as a point of reference to gauge the decision-making aptitudes of foreign policy makers. These aptitudes, moreover, can be delineated and measured by alternative cognitive theories. The end result of this analytical process is the formulation of a typology of decision-making aptitudes with significant theoretical implications.

From Attribution Theory to Cognitive Consistency Theory

Rationality in foreign policy making entails collecting the information necessary to define the nature of an international problem, isolating and ranking the affected values, identifying the alternatives and the costs and benefits the implementation of each could elicit, and choosing the option with the highest expected utility. In the 1950s, Herbert Simon argued that because it is humanly impossible to assess all pertinent information and to consider all relevant alternatives and their potential consequences, decisions always fall short of the ideal. His suggestion was to recognize that rationality is bounded.[17]

A similar conception drives *attribution theory*. As a theory, it is defined not by one perspective but by competing models that differ in their descriptions of cognitive processes, information used, and outcomes. All these models, however, assume that individuals formulate causal explanations of behavior which, in turn, help shape their reactions.[18]

In 1967, Harold Kelley, one of the best-known advocates of attribution theory, proposed that the decision maker be viewed as a lay scientist, as an individual who tries to "infer causes for the effects he observes."[19] According to Kelley, the lay attributor, in an attempt to attribute causes to events of the form "Actor responds in fashion to situation A" will respond to three types of information: distinctiveness, consistency, and consensus. Distinctiveness information refers to the analyst's attempt to compare the relationship between an effect and various causes.[20] The second type of information, consistency information, focuses on the analyst's attempt to measure how often the assumed cause precedes the effect in question. And the third type, consensus information, refers to the analyst's effort to establish whether other subjects respond in the same fashion to the presumed cause.[21] Richard Nisbett and Lee Ross carried the metaphor of the naive scientist a step further. They proposed that the analyst tries, just like the regular scientist, to describe accurately an event or object, characterize sample data, generalize from the sample data to the population of subjects or events, measure the covariation between subjects or events, propose causal explanations, predict the future, and test theories.[22]

Attribution theorists acknowledge that the decision maker often tries to confirm his hypothesis by searching for evidence that is consistent with his expectation. This form of behavior, they note, needs to be ascribed not to an assumed tendency by the decision maker to focus only on information that confirms his expectations, but to his unawareness that the most effective and systematic manner to gauge the soundness of a proposition is by attempting to falsify it.[23]

The depiction of the analyst as a "naive" scientist stands closest to the model of the rational decision maker and in opposition to that which characterizes him as a "consistency seeker."[24] In the 1950s, various social psychologists proposed that humans lack the psychological maturity required to carry out the tasks associated with a rational decision-making process. When humans process and interpret information, they are not just attempting to understand a problem and formulate a solution; they are also trying to ensure that in the process their beliefs, feelings, and cognitions remain mutually consistent.[25]

A consistent structure is one in which "all relations among 'good elements' [i.e. those that are positively valued] are positive (or null), all relations among 'bad elements' [i.e. those that are negatively valued] are positive (or null), and all relations among good and bad elements are negative (or null)."[26] This model, thus, perceives the mind not as a machine in quest of meaning and validity, but as a veritable inference-making instrument that actively manipulates the information it receives to create a consistent structure out of an ambiguous reality.[27]

Faced with uncertainty, contend cognitive consistency theorists, the analyst imposes on reality a structure that makes events or subjects have a clear, coherent meaning. Through the use of categorical rather than probable judgments, the analyst convinces himself that he can predict decision outcomes and does not need to evaluate other alternatives. Such a judgment is generally derived from a reinforcing experience. The process is identified as the *assumption of a single outcome calculation*. Moreover, faced with a problem involving conflicting values, the decision maker separates them and makes choices in terms of only one value, without estimating how the other values may be affected. This predisposition on the part of the analyst is known as the *assumption of value separation*.[28]

Between attribution theory and cognitive consistency theory lie schema theory and one of its derivatives, Robert Abelson's theory of cognitive scripts.[29] According to schema theorists, the decision maker, overwhelmed by sensations and information, seeks to understand the world without using inordinate amounts of energy and time. He compresses reality by matching present experiences with schemas he has stored in his memory from past events. Schema theory shares with attribution theory the assumption that the individual is not driven by an internal need to maintain a balance between beliefs and actions, but has fewer illusions about his analytical capabilities. According to schema theory, the individual commits errors when he handles information not because he does not know better (although he may not), but because he lacks the time and energy and his mental capabilities are limited.

A cognitive script refers to a sequence of events that tells a story, is known well by foreign policy makers, and is recorded in their memories in the form of a stereotype. Abelson differentiates between episodic and categoric scripts. An episodic script is based on the analysis of a single experience which is defined by a sequence of events. In the early 1950, for instance, analysts at the Department of State stored in their memories the "Yenan Way" script, in which radical agrarian reforms instituted in China were believed to have contributed to the creation of the Chinese communist system. An episodic script may or may not be generalized to form a categorical script. When a number of similar experiences are structured by analogous sequences of events, foreign policy makers "may generalize from the common features to form one categorical script." From the Yenan Way script and other related incidents, foreign policy makers in the 1950s created the categorical script: "radical agrarian reforms are the prelude to the birth of communist regimes." The designing of a categorical script, however, is not always preceded by a number of similar past experiences. One single costly incident can pressure foreign policy makers to transform an episodic script into a categorical one. Lyndon Johnson's determination to ensure that the Dominican Republic in 1965 would not become a "second Cuba" attests to this possibility.[30]

Let us assume that the ideal foreign policy-making process involves the systematic collection of information to define the real nature of an international problem, the isolation and ranking of values affected by the problem, the identification of possible alternatives along with their expected costs and benefits, and the selection of the alternative with the highest expected utility. Then, in order to develop a typology of decision-making aptitudes based on the arguments elicited from the different cognitive theories, it is necessary to focus on how each responds to the aforementioned tasks. It has been proposed already that of the three cognitive models, attribution theory comes the closest to the ideal assumption, with cognitive consistency theory standing at the opposite end of the spectrum. More specifically, this signifies that when attribution, schema and cognitive consistency theories are compared, the first one has greater expectations than the other two about an individual's decision-making capabilities.

From attribution theory it can be inferred that the decision maker first gathers whatever information he needs to describe the nature of the problem and to identify its affected values. Subsequently, he studies a variety of alternatives by looking at sample data of past events involving the originator of the problem and other actors entangled in similar situations. In particular, he tries to ascertain whether his adversary was prone to respond in the same way, regardless of the policy he was confronted with, or in different ways depending on the policy; and if the latter was to be the case, how strong his tendency was to react to the same policy in the same way. He then attempts to establish whether the present problem maker's past responses to the various policies were unique or concurred with the responses of other past problem makers. The decision-making process in this case is not obstructed by the need to keep his beliefs, feelings, and cognitions mutually consistent, nor by a desire to minimize uncertainty in order to assuage certain insecurities. The principal obstacle is the decision maker's own inability to understand that the most rational way to evaluate his adversary's behavioral pattern is by referring not to the cases that fit nicely with his initial expectation but to those that, at face value, are likely to fail to meet his expectation. In other words, he does not realize that failure by a least likely case to falsify his argument will strengthen the soundness of his hypothesis.

Schema theory, with its emphasis on scripts, posits a different description of the decision-making process. Burdened by the need to save energy and time, and by his inability to process vast amounts of information, the decision maker relies on a script to define an international problem. He may use either an episodic or categorical script to define the problem, but in either case his definition results from conclusions he inferred from one or more notable, analogous situations. The content of the script he uses to define the problem, moreover, bounds the range of values he believes are pertinent and the type of alternatives he evaluates, and affects his final policy choice.

Thus, according to schema theory, the decision maker does not rely on a quasi-scientific approach to problem solving. His definition of an international problem is the result not of an attempt to contrast competing explanations of past actions by the problem maker and other actors, but of a script he derived from a very narrow set of cases, and recorded deep in his memory because of their political, social, economic, or moral significance. This same decision maker does not decide on a policy by evaluating past responses by the problem maker and other parties in order to understand what values are at stake and how different alternatives may affect them. Instead, he searches for a script that enables him to capture the analogous relationships between a narrow set of consequential past responses and the response he believes is required by the new problem.[31]

The least rational form of behavior expected from a decision maker is that explained by cognitive consistency theory. The need by a decision maker to avoid inconsistencies and to give an uncertain situation an unchallenged, well-defined form, prompts him to disregard potentially valuable information. This need, moreover, induces him to evaluate only those alternatives that do not contradict his preconceptions and to disregard the possibility that some of his alternatives may impact negatively on a few of his values. This faulty process also imposes itself on the policy selection task. The decision maker opts for the alternative that most strongly reinforces his preconceptions and dismisses any remaining doubts about the outcome. Under cognitive consistency theory, thus, rationality is undercut not by the absence of information about how to garner knowledge, want of intellectual capacity, nor inclination to conserve energy and time on the part of the decision maker. The culprit is his psychological insecurity—his inability to accept that uncertainty in the international arena is a common phenomenon, that his preconceptions sometimes are wrong, and that his preferred options are not always the best ones.

The three theories, as described, assume that an individual's decision making aptitude remains constant. The general assumption is that a person who rationalizes according to the precepts of attribution theory is unlikely to suddenly be dominated by a tremendous need to keep his beliefs, feelings, and cognitions mutually consistent; and, vice versa, that an individual who rationalizes according to the precepts of cognitive consistency theory is unlikely to all at once free himself from the need to maintain cognitive balance. This assumption, although appealing because of its parsimonious nature, may need to be explored more carefully. Events with great consequences are bound to have considerable effects on the decision-making aptitudes of foreign policy leaders. John F. Kennedy's decision to topple Fidel Castro's government in 1961, for instance, can be explained by cognitive consistency theory.[32] The same theory, however, cannot be used to explain his actions during the Cuban missile crisis. In 1962, Kennedy sought to ensure that he would not err during the decision-making process as he had the previous year. Thus, instead of assuming that the decision-making aptitudes of foreign policy makers remain constant through time, this analysis assumes that past experiences, positive or negative, can alter them.

Groupthink and Decision-Making Aptitudes

Momentous decisions are made typically by individuals who interact as members of a small decision-making group.

The president surrounds himself with a small number of individuals who keep him informed about the latest important developments both at home and abroad, suggest and evaluate potential policies, and act as a sounding board for his ideas. Students of foreign policy making have proposed that the size, membership, and role structure of the group can have a significant effect not just on how policies are formulated, but also on their quality. Irving Janis, for instance, writes:

> [T]he advantages of having decisions made by groups are often lost because of psychological pressures that arise when the members work closely together, share the same values, and above all face a crisis situation in which everybody is subjected to stresses that generate a strong need for affiliation.[33]

The intent of this section is not to rehash an old argument, but to ascertain whether it is imperative to account for a decision-making group's dynamic when analyzing the reasoning process of its principal parties.

According to Irving Janis and Leon Mann, the constitution of a decision-making group can affect the way its members search for and process information, survey objectives and alternatives, examine the risks of a preferred choice, reappraise alternatives, and work out contingency plans.[34] A group that is highly cohesive, emotionally and functionally dependent on its leader, insulated from other groups, and deficient in methodical procedures for search and appraisal is likely to reflect eight symptoms of groupthink. By "groupthink", Janis means "a mode of thinking that people engage in when they are deeply involved in a cohesive in-group, when the members' striving for unanimity override their motivation to realistically appraise alternative courses of action."[35] A group that reflects the symptoms of groupthink will have its self-appointed mind guards. It will rationalize collectively, develop illusions of invulnerability and unanimity, believe in its inherent morality, view other groups as adversaries and as being less capable, tolerate only self-censorship, and pressure internal dissenters to conform. When such a group is faced with a high stress problem, it will be inclined to conduct a poor information search, process only that information that confirms its members' beliefs and expectations, and carry out an incomplete survey of objectives and alternatives. It will tend to not examine the risks behind its preferred choice, not reappraise alternatives, and not work out contingency plans.

Notwithstanding the fact that groupthink, as a theoretical construct, has been challenged by a wide range of analysts, it is helpful to investigate the conditions under which it could come into being. Every president, as Alexander George notes, "faces the task of deciding how to organize and manage foreign-policy making in his administration."[36] George adds that the way a president organizes and manages his foreign policy making is a function of his sense of efficacy as it relates to management and decision-making tasks, informational needs and ways of acquiring and using information and advice, attitude to the give-and-take of politics, and tolerance for conflict among his advisers. In other words, George's basic postulate is that the president dictates the structure of the group that helps him formulate policies which, in turn, affects the quality of the foreign policy-making process.[37] If this is the case, then it would seem redundant to analyze both a president's reasoning process and the structure of the group that advises him. However, rather than accepting the logic of the challenge just postulated, this study will attempt to evaluate its validity by focusing on both the reasoning processes of Bush and his principal advisers and the structure of the group that encompassed them.

Chapter Three

A Preventable Surprise

Two Weeks to Surprise

One of the primary functions of any intelligence analyst is to give meaning to imprecise information. On 16 July 1990, Walter P. Lang, the Pentagon's senior civilian intelligence analyst for the Middle East and South Asia region, noticed something unusual as he studied the latest satellite photos.[1] They revealed that a brigade of one of Iraq's most powerful tank divisions was deployed close to Kuwait's northern border, and that equipment belonging to the Republican Guard, Saddam Hussein's most feared and powerful elite unit, was being loaded on trains.

Lang knew that he needed more information before he could write Lt. Gen. Harry E. Soyster, his superior and director of the Defense Intelligence Agency, a report explaining what he believed Saddam planned to do with his newly deployed forces. But he was also aware that he could not afford to take lightly what he had noticed on the photographs. Part of his task was to place the military logic behind Iraq's deployment of Soviet-made T-72 tanks in the context of Saddam's repeated demands that Kuwait adhere to the oil quota set up by the Organization of Petroleum Exporting Countries (OPEC). Lang remembered Saddam's threat at the Arab summit held in Baghdad at the end of May 1990. The Iraqi leader had complained that overproduction of oil by some Gulf states had caused prices to plummet from the agreed-upon price of $18 a barrel to $7 a barrel. "War," Saddam had noted, "takes place sometimes through soldiers and damage is inflicted by explosives, killings, or coup attempts. At other times, war is launched through economic means. To those who do not mean to wage war against Iraq, I say that this is a kind of war against Iraq."[2] He had also warned that Iraq was determined not to tolerate "any more pressure."[3]

Lang's information needs were met almost immediately. On 19 July, new photographs revealed that Iraq had deployed three of its tank divisions and some thirty-five thousand men within ten to thirty miles of the Kuwaiti border.[4] This new data, however, posed a major challenge to the intelligence analyst. His immediate problem was how to balance the latest signals emanating from the Iraqi-Kuwaiti border with an earlier assessment by U.S. intelligence which had concluded that although Saddam Hussein wanted to become the Gulf region's dominant figure, the costs absorbed by his country during its war against Iran would restrain him from using force in the immediate future.[5]

In his first report, Lang chose not to contest the status quo. He informed his superior about the troop movement, noted that it was unusual, and warned that it was typical of Saddam to rehearse operations and battles in vacant areas before engaging his tanks. At this stage, however, he was not ready to conclude that the Iraqi leader would attack Kuwait.

Others derived similar conclusions. Gen. Colin Powell, chairman of the Joint Chiefs of Staff (JCS), was troubled by Iraq's actions, but not alarmed. The JCS's director of operations, Lt. Gen. Thomas W. Kelly, argued that Saddam was merely attempting to pressure Kuwait to acquiesce to his demands, and that he might take only an oil field or the two small islands in the Persian Gulf that Iraq had been aspiring to control for quite some time. And finally, Gen. H. Norman Schwarzkopf, who as commander of the Central Command was responsible for overseeing U.S. military interests in the Middle East and Southwest Asia, concluded that the most Iraq might do was to launch a punitive but limited attack against Kuwait.

Iraq's deployment of troops continued. Eleven days after he had uncovered Iraq's first tank deployment, Lang counted eight divisions deployed north of Kuwait, along with one hundred thousand troops. The Bush administration, however, was still unwilling to alter its assessment. Powell, for instance, took notice of a cable sent by the U.S. ambassador to Iraq, April Glaspie. In it, the ambassador referred to her meeting with Saddam; from his words she had inferred that he might still be able to iron out his differences with Kuwait without resorting to force.[6] Powell was encouraged also by what he heard from the Saudi ambassador to the United States, Prince Bandar bin Sultan. Bandar had stated that the feeling in the Middle East was that Iraq would not invade Kuwait.[7] Moreover, as a military man, Powell placed great emphasis on the fact that Iraq had not executed many of the steps typically taken by a state getting ready to launch an attack, such as augmenting the communications network in the area, putting in place artillery stocks and other munitions necessary for offensive action, and increasing the supply line. Top officials of the White House and the State Department shared Powell's optimism. The CIA, in turn, although concerned about Iraq's military buildup, believed that it would be unprecedented for one Arab state to attack another.

U.S. optimism experienced a major crack on 30 July. Walter Lang, after carefully reevaluating the data and reassessing what he knew about Saddam Hussein, wrote to his superior, Lieutenant General Soyster:

> [Saddam Hussein] has created the capability to overrun all of Kuwait and all of Eastern Saudi Arabia.

If he attacks, given his disposition, we will have no warning.

I do not believe he is bluffing. I have looked at his personality profile. He doesn't know how to bluff. It is not in his pattern of behavior.

I fear that Kuwait will be so stiff-necked in answering his demands that they will not fulfill his minimal requirements.

In short, Saddam Hussein has moved a force disproportionate to the task at hand, [and] if it is to bluff then there is only one answer: he intends to use it.[8]

Soyster disagreed with Lang's analysis. Nevertheless, he submitted it to Secretary of Defense Richard Cheney and Colin Powell. Both believed Lang's conclusion was premature.[9]

Saddam's military deployment continued. By 1 August, U.S. satellite photographs showed that Iraq's three armored divisions had been moved within three miles off the Kuwaiti border, with two positioned close to the main four-lane highway leading into the center of Kuwait, and the third standing on its western side. Lang immediately concluded that Iraq was about to launch an attack. The CIA concurred with Lang's assessment by contending that all indicators pointed to an impending invasion.

Neither the DIA nor the CIA was able to convince Powell or Cheney. Powell acknowledged that it was difficult to disregard the latest data, but he also believed that because Iraq was being ruled by a totalitarian regime and the U.S. lacked good human sources inside the government that could assess Saddam's intentions, it was still too early to conclude that he planned to attack. Furthermore, Powell could not understand why Saddam would use some one hundred thousand troops if he planned to invade Kuwait, when he could achieve the same objective with fewer forces. Cheney shared Powell's skepticism. He argued that there was no way to determine whether the Iraqi leader was planning to go to war or was merely attempting to scare the Kuwaitis. His analysis was almost a replica of the briefing he and the Joint Chiefs had received from Schwarzkopf.

They were all wrong, except Lang and the CIA. At 9:00 P.M. on 1 August, Cheney was informed that Iraqi tanks had rolled into Kuwait and were racing towards Kuwait City. The United States, with the most sophisticated intelligence system in the world and with an abundance of information suggesting that Saddam Hussein planned to invade Kuwait, was surprised by his action.

The Logic of Surprise Avoidance

Frederick the Great once declared that it was pardonable to be defeated in war, but not to be surprised. In the early 1980s, a reputable intelligence and decision-making analyst challenged Frederick's contention, proposing that any party intent on attaining surprise can succeed, because the requirements of a successful strategy of deception are not overly demanding.[10]

Both overstated their arguments. Because there is no sure method for avoiding surprise, victims of surprise must sometimes be pardoned. And conversely, because the successful implementation of a strategy of deception can be very demanding, would-be surprisers do not always succeed. The Bush administration, however, cannot plead for forgiveness. Saddam Hussein did not attempt to achieve surprise, and U.S. officials had more than sufficient evidence to conclude that an invasion of Kuwait was probable.

A strategy of surprise is the result of conscious, carefully calculated decisions made prior to the outbreak of overt hostilities. At its most basic level, it entails the deliberate cultivation by one party of misunderstanding on the part of another.[11] The main task faced by the would-be surpriser is to make the victim select a false or unfavorable alternative. The would-be aggressor can achieve either end by introducing ambiguity to the situation or by encouraging the victim to formulate a solution to his predicament different from the "correct" solution.[12]

The would-be surpriser can choose from six dimensions of surprise, some of which he can use concurrently. If possible, he will attempt to disguise both his intention and rationale; that is, he will try to prevent his victim from learning what he wants to do and why. Moreover, he may take major steps to conceal his state's true aggregate economic and military strength, and the type, size, location, movement, and readiness of his military forces. Coupled with this dimension is his need to conceal the military doctrine that will guide the operation. And finally, whenever possible, a would-be surpriser will make an effort to prevent his victim from learning that he is the target and when he will be attacked.[13]

Saddam Hussein did not seek to achieve surprise in any of these ways. To understand his strategy, we must begin with a speech he delivered on 24 February 1990, while attending a meeting in Amman, Jordan, with its country's ruler, King Hussein, and President Hosni Mubarak of Egypt. In the speech, which was broadcasted on Jordanian television, the Iraqi leader warned that because of the Soviet Union's waning power, the United States could become the Middle East's hegemon.

> The country that will have the greatest influence in the region, through the Arab Gulf and its oil, will maintain its superiority as a superpower without an equal to compete with it. This means that if the Gulf people, along with all Arabs, are not careful, the Arab Gulf region will be governed by the wishes of the United States.[14]

The speech so angered President Mubarak, the United States's main Arab ally in the Middle East, that it may have led him to break up the meeting a day before its scheduled completion.

Saddam did not moderate his behavior with the passage of time. On 1 April, in a widely publicized talk, he bragged about his country's chemical weapons capability and threatened to burn half of Israel if it attacked Iraq. "[W]e will make the fire eat up half of Israel, if it tries to do anything against Iraq."[15] The Bush administration called the speech "inflammatory, irresponsible, and outrageous."[16]

A few days later, Saddam asked King Fahd of Saudi Arabia to send a trusted representative to Iraq to discuss the latest developments in the region. In a meeting with Bandar bin Sultan, Saddam made it clear that he would not attack Israel, but that he needed a guarantee from the United States that Israel would not attack Iraq. Prince Bandar returned to Washington and delivered Saddam's message to President Bush on 9 April. Bush, during his conversation with Bandar, noted that he could not understand why Saddam would threaten Israel if he had no intention of attacking it. The meeting ended without Bush extending any assurances to the Saudi ambassador. Bush and Bandar held a second meeting in mid-April, at which time the president agreed to talk to the Israelis. When contacted by the White House, the Israelis made it clear that they would not attack Iraq so long as Iraq did not attack Israel. Saddam received Israel's assurance directly from the United States.

For a time, Saddam seemed to have feared that Israel might exploit Iraq's weak standing in the region after its unsuccessful war against Iran, and sought reassurance from the United States that Israel would not attack his country.[17] However, his behavior and his rationale for demanding that Israel commit itself not to attack Iraq, also parallels the strategy adopted by one of his great heroes—Adolf Hitler—some 51 years earlier.

On 23 August 1939, the world learned that Germany and the Soviet Union had signed a nonaggression pact. About a week later, Germany invaded Poland. The invasion persuaded Great Britain and France that they could no longer tolerate Hitler's action and, thus declared war on Germany. But Hitler was prepared. As he deployed his forces against Germany's two old adversaries, he knew that at least for some time he would not have to worry about fighting a two-front war—the Soviets had been bought off.[18]

Saddam achieved a similar objective in April 1990.[19] Before
he could move against Kuwait, the Iraqi leader had to receive
a commitment from the Israelis, backed by the United States,
that they would not move against Iraq as he exposed its
western flank.[20] When the assurance was extended, Saddam
waited less than a month to express his determination to take
action against Kuwait unless its government met his demands.
As already noted, at the Arab League summit meeting in
Baghdad in May, Saddam warned that he and his people would
not tolerate much longer the "economic war" launched against
his country by some Arab states.Then in the middle of July
he moved his troops close to the Kuwaiti border, taking no
measures to conceal his action[21], the number of troops he
planned to use to attack Kuwait, and the military doctrine
that he would rely on. Fully aware that the United States had
the technology to monitor the type, size, location, and
movement of his troops, Saddam could have attempted to
camouflage them. But from 16 July on, he deployed his forces
as if he were attempting to make certain that Washington
would know precisely what he would do. Moreover, he made
sure that Washington would be able to estimate the time of
the attack; his troops had moved swiftly towards the border
and had assumed in a very short time the posture typically
adopted by forces ready to launch an attack.

All of this became evident to Lang. On 1 August, he
concluded that "Saddam was being very deliberate." In Lang's
mind, the "armored units could not more vividly advertise
their intent. It was as if a gun had been loaded and aimed,
and a finger put on the trigger."[22] And yet, Lang's superiors
did not share his confidence. They argued that the deployment
of forces could mean that the Iraqi leader planned either to
invade Kuwait or to pressure its leaders to acquiesce to his
demands. Their reluctance to accept Lang's assessment was
completely unwarranted.

The estimation of intention is often assumed to be an
extremely complex task. To evaluate an opponent's intention
"the analyst needs a theory or model of that adversary's
behavioral style and approach to calculating political action."[23]

Several obstacles stand in the way of the analyst's attempt to design a theory or model of his adversary. First, there is the tendency to depict as irrational any unusual behavior by leaders belonging to a different culture. Cultural dissonance often leads an analyst to miscalculate the risks leaders adhering to a different set of values are willing to absorb.[24] Second, there is the question of data. A potential victim does not always face a leader with a rich history that can be analyzed in great detail. Third, there is the problem of determining how the belief system of an adversary mediates his responses with regard to different situations. And fourth, there is the difficulty of assessing an opponent's mode of calculating utilities. The analyst faces the unenviable task of determining how an adversary ranks his preferences, and whether his present ranking corresponds with past rankings.[25]

Based on the above argument it may be tempting to conclude that, as it is so difficult to estimate an actor's intention, would-be surprisers have a considerable advantage over their victims. And yet, intended victims of surprise have not always been surprised by their adversaries' decisions to attack. As a would-be surpriser begins to display his forces, he increases significantly the victim's chances of recognizing that he may become the target of an attack.[26]

An actor's preparation for war does not signal that he intends to actually go to war. Failure to respond to an actor's preparation for war, however, can invite attack. In July 1990, Iran and Kuwait restored diplomatic relations. On 16 July, Iraq signaled its displeasure with Kuwait's behavior by accusing the latter of stealing some $2.4 billion of oil drilled from the Rumalieh field and warned, by deploying its troops, that such an action would not be tolerated. Secretary of Defense Cheney responded immediately to the threat with the warning that the Bush administration would "take seriously any threats to U.S. interests or U.S. friends in the region."[27]

Saddam responded immediately to the secretary of defense's notice. Wondering whether Cheney's statement reflected a commitment on the part of the United States to try to deter Iraq, the Iraqi leader met with U.S. Ambassador April Glaspie on 25 July.

For Saddam, the meeting was crucial. He began by emphasizing the need for mutual understanding. He noted that when the interests between two countries "are limited and relations are not old, then there isn't a deep understanding and mistakes could have a negative effect. *Sometimes the effect of an error can be larger than the error itself."*[28] He continued by trying to clarify why he was concerned about the drop in the price of oil. "[W]hen planned and deliberate policy forces the price of oil down without good commercial reasons, then that means another war against Iraq. . . . Kuwait and the U.A.E. were at the front of this policy aimed at lowering Iraq's position and depriving its people of higher economic standards." He then added that the United States had to "have a better understanding of the situation and declare who it wants to have relations with and who its enemies are."

Ambassador Glaspie went out of her way to emphasize that the Bush administration was determined to find a way to improve the relationship between the United States and Iraq. She began by stating that she had "direct instruction from the President to seek better relations with Iraq," and by apologiding for how some members of the American media had depicted the Iraqi leader.[29] She did make it a point, however, to ask Saddam to explain what he hoped to achieve by deploying his forces so close to the Kuwaiti border. "[W]e can only see that you have deployed massive troops in the south. Normally that would not be any of our business. But when this happens in the context of what you said on your national day, then when we read the details in the two letters of the foreign minister, then when we see the Iraqi point of view that the measures taken by the U.A.E. and Kuwait is, in the final analysis, parallel to military aggression against Iraq, then it would be reasonable for me to be concerned. And for this reason, I received an instruction to ask you, in the spirit of friendship—not in the spirit of confrontation— regarding your intentions."[30]

Saddam's response should have left very few doubts. He made it clear that he understood the concern of the United

States, but then reiterated that he wanted "others to know that [Iraq's] patience [was] running out regarding their action," and that although Iraq was not an aggressor, it did not "accept aggression either." Then he added that he had no intention of doing "anything until we meet with them [the Kuwaitis]. When we meet and we see that there is hope, then nothing will happen. But if we are unable to find a solution, then it will be natural that Iraq will not accept death, even though wisdom is above everything else."

Saddam's summoning of the U.S. ambassador and his demand that she state specifically whether the Bush administration stood with Iraq or with Kuwait indicates that he wanted to know how Washington would respond to an invasion of Kuwait by Iraq. Following Cheney's warning that the United States would "take seriously" any threat to its friends, the U.S. ambassador could have made it clear to Saddam that Washington would not tolerate any type of violation of Kuwait's sovereignty. And yet, the United States, through its ambassador, missed the opportunity.[31]

Two explanations can be elicited for Washington's failure to make its position clear. The conspiratorial argument would contend that Washington expected Saddam to invade Kuwait and did little to deter him because U.S. foreign policy makers saw the event as a perfect opportunity to revitalize the image of the United States as a world hegemon. With the cold war coming to an end and Germany and Japan moving closer to center stage, leaders in Washington concluded that they needed a new cause to counteract their challenge. The military, moreover, hoped for an invasion to display its capabilities and as an example for the need for continued military expenditures.

This argument does not withstand scrutiny on three counts. First, as will be explained later in greater detail, for quite some time the United States had been attempting to improve its relationship with Iraq. Second, the second-most-important foreign policy maker in the United States, Secretary of State James Baker III, and the Pentagon's most powerful military official, Gen. Colin Powell, did not favor the use of force against Iraq following its invasion of Kuwait. Both advocated giving the international economic embargo time to have an effect before deciding whether to use force. And third, the evidence available thus far shows quite clearly that the principal foreign policy makers in Washington seriously doubted that Saddam Hussein would invade Kuwait. It is at this juncture that we can finally begin to unravel the reason that the United States was surprised.

Preconceptions and Misperceptions

As a world power, the United States monitors and evaluates vast amounts of information coming from different parts of the world. Although Washington possesses major resources to process great quantities of data, its central foreign policy makers lack the time and interest to address every pending problem. The Middle East, a volatile area with the ingredients to engulf the world in deadly crises, has preoccupied Washington's core foreign policy makers for years. But in mid-1990, developments in the Middle East had difficulty competing with events in Eastern Europe and the Soviet Union. The initial excitement generated by the crumbling of the iron curtain was being drowned by the emergence of a myriad of new problems. At first there was elation when the Soviet Union admitted it could no longer compete in the arms race with the United States, when East and West Germany became one, and when Eastern Europe began to experiment with democracy and capitalism. But euphoria was soon replaced by the realization that these changes were freeing contradictory forces powerful enough to create havoc in the international system. With their eyes and minds fixed on these developments, the leading players within the Bush administration had difficulty altering their priorities. Eventually, however, they had to; Saddam's actions had became too blatant. The U.S. leaders' mistake was in misreading those actions.

The principal culprits were Scowcroft, Cheney, Powell, and Schwarzkopf. All four knew what Saddam had said and what his troops had done. They had all read Lang's memo detailing his rationale for believing that the Iraqi leader planned to invade Kuwait. Ultimately, however, each found his own reason to disregard the tactical evidence that seemed so obvious to the DIA analyst. To understand their mind-set in 1990, it is first necessary to paint with broad strokes some developments in the Middle East prior to the 1990 invasion.

On 23 January 1980, President Jimmy Carter, in his State of the Union address to a joint session of Congress declared:

> Any attempt by an outside force to gain control of the Persian Gulf region will be regarded as an assault on the vital interests of the United States of America and such an assault will be repelled by any means necessary, including military force.[32]

This warning, often referred to as the Carter Doctrine, was advanced in response to the Soviet invasion of Afghanistan in December 1979, and was modeled on the Truman Doctrine designed in 1946. As explained by Carter's national security adviser, Zbigniew Brzezinski, just as the threat to Greece and Turkey by the Soviet Union had demanded a firm response on the part of the Truman administration, so the "collapse of Iran and the growing vulnerability of Saudi Arabia dictated the need for a wide strategic response by the Carter administration."[33]

Throughout 1980, the national security adviser tried to give the Carter Doctrine a more precise form. Worried that the absence of a "regional security framework" in the Middle East might tempt the Soviet Union to escalate its involvement in the region, Brzezinski proposed to the principal foreign policy makers in the Carter administration that the United States set up bases on Arab soil and that nations in the area friendly to the United States augment their military capabilities.[34] His concern seemed justified. In August of that same year, U.S. intelligence reports indicated that the Soviet

Union was moving troops to its border with Iran in preparation for a possible intervention. On 5 September, at a meeting at the White House, the national security adviser suggested that Washington send a tough message to Moscow warning that the United States would retaliate with military force should Soviet troops enter Iran. Secretary of State Edmund Muskie, concerned that the crisis could result in a war with the Soviet Union, warned that the U.S. Congress would not risk a nuclear war to protect 11 percent of U.S. oil supplies. He then recommended sending Moscow a stiff message that excluded the threat of military force. Jimmy Carter followed Muskie's advice.[35]

Although it is unclear how the Carter administration would have responded to a Soviet invasion of Iran, its general apprehension was the by-product of two long-standing interests. Since the end of the Second World War, the United States had sought to ensure access by the industrialized world to the Middle East's vast oil resources and to prevent the Soviet Union from gaining political or military control over such resources.[36]

These interests were reaffirmed in 1981, when the Reagan administration moved into the White House. Although the invasion feared by Brzezinski never materialized, and news from the Middle East was dominated by the war that had been raging between Iran and Iraq, the new administration came to power determined to battle Soviet influence in the region. In April 1981, Secretary of State Alexander Haig traveled to the Middle East hoping to persuade Gulf nations and neighboring states to enter into bilateral agreements with Washington that would formally permit U.S. forces to be stationed on Arab soil. The Arab states, contending that the Soviet threat was not strong enough to warrant such agreements, rejected Haig's proposal.[37] Some of them feared not the Soviet Union but Iran and the effects its fundamentalist revolution might have throughout the Middle East. Saudi Arabia, cognizant that it lacked the means to protect itself and convinced that the presence of U.S. troops would help germinate internal discord, committed itself to expanding its military force and arsenal. The Reagan administration, realizing that it had no choice but to accept Saudi Arabia's stand, worked hard to persuade the U.S. Congress that it would be in the interest of the United States to sell Saudi Arabia the arms it had requested. After a bitter debate, the U.S. Congress approved the sale of $8.5 billion in arms to Saudi Arabia.

This victory, however, did not prove to be significant. Faced with a Soviet Union unable to affect in any major way the course of events in the Middle East, due to its inability to extricate itself from the costly war in Afghanistan, the Reagan administration continued with its struggle to generate a Middle East policy. But it soon learned, as other administrations had in years past, that the Middle East is not always impressed by the stamina and power of the United States. The Reagan administration was hit hard particularly by its failure in 1982 and 1983 to help resolve the crisis in Lebanon.

The war in Lebanon, which had begun in 1975, took a bad turn in April 1981, when Syria, led by Hafez Assad, bombed the Christian town of Zahle in the Bekka Valley. The town had been infiltrated by forces loyal to the Maronite Christian leader Bashin Gemayel, who was known to have close ties to the United States and Israel. Hafez Assad ordered the attack, hoping to prevent the Israelis from establishing a permanent presence in Lebanon that could threaten Syria. Shortly afterwards, Israel shot down two Syrian helicopters. But the worst was yet to come. On 17 July, Israel launched an air raid on Beirut, killing some three hundred persons and injuring approximately eight hundred. From then on, conditions in Lebanon deteriorated rapidly; and so did U.S.-Israeli relations.[38]

On 6 June 1982, Israel launched Operation Peace in Galilee. The operation entailed invading Lebanon for the purpose of driving the PLO back from the Israeli border "so that all of [the Israeli] civilians in the region of Galilee [would] be set free of the permanent threat to their lives."[39] Israel's invasion was followed by an increase in violence in Lebanon. These events provoked a major decision on the part of the

Reagan administration, but one that did not receive the unanimous endorsement from its principal policy makers.

In early June 1982, State Department and National Security Council officials discussed the idea of creating a multinational peacekeeping force to bring the fighting in Lebanon to an end. The concept was not endorsed by Pentagon officials. On 19 June, the chairman of the Joint Chiefs of Staff, General John W. Vessey, wrote a memo to Secretary of Defense Caspar Weinberger, urging him to tell Reagan that it would "be very unwise for the U.S. to find itself in a position where it had to put its forces between the Israelis and the Arabs."[40] On 2 July, however, Reagan accepted the argument of his departing Secretary of State Alexander Haig and his special envoy to the Middle East Philip Habib, that if the United States expressed its willingness to commit forces to a multinational peacekeeping force in Lebanon, the commitment would make the creation of such a force possible. The creation of the force, in turn, would halt the fighting in Lebanon and give the United States greater leverage in its negotiations with Israel.[41]

U.S., French, and Italian forces were interposed between thirty thousand Israeli troops and fifteen thousand Syrian and Palestinian soldiers. The deployment of the multinational peacekeeping force seemed to have its intended effect. By 1 September, the last of the Syrian and Palestinian forces had left, and Lebanon had its own government. Washington wasted little time in removing its own troops. By 10 September, it had evacuated the U.S. Marines to their ships near Lebanon's shores.

Not all of Reagan's advisers applauded this decision. Officials at the Pentagon, especially Weinberger and Vessey, after having failed to persuade Reagan not to deploy U.S. forces in Lebanon, went out of their way to ensure that the mission would be defined as narrowly and as specifically as possible. Furthermore, as soon as they felt that the military objective had been achieved, they pressed Reagan to withdraw the U.S. Marines. The secretary of defense was determined to ensure that Lebanon would not become a "second Vietnam." As noted by his military assistant at the Pentagon, Colin Powell, Weinberger "never wanted to ever preside over anything like a Vietnam involvement by U.S forces. . . ."[42] Shultz and Habib, on the other hand, expressed their strong misgivings about pulling the troops out. They believed that by keeping its forces in Lebanon the United States would help prevent the further eruption of violence and might be able to persuade the contending parties to reach a negotiated settlement.

On 14 September, just four days after the U.S. Marines had been evacuated, Shultz's and Habib's apprehensions became reality. Nine days before he was to be sworn in as president of Lebanon, Christian leader Bashil Gemayel was assassinated. The following day, Israeli troops occupied West Beirut. Four days later, Reagan announced the formation of a new multinational force. Once again his advisers failed to agree on whether it would be wise to have U.S. Marines deployed on Lebanon soil. But this time the stay would be longer and costlier.

Throughout part of 1983, the decision-making process in Washington lacked guidance. "We were all struggling in the dark," states Geoffrey Kemp, the Middle East expert at the National Security Council. "The president had pretty good practical instincts, but there was so much indecision in the administration, so much conflict between State and Defense. The net result of the indecision was chaos."[43] The struggle, as before, was between two camps. One camp, made up by Weinberger and the Joint Chiefs of Staff, kept warning about the dangers of keeping the U.S. Marines in Lebanon's hostile environment. The other camp, led by Secretary of State Shultz, "saw the U.S. forces as a flexible tool of diplomacy" and viewed the top military brass as "cautious doves willing to take flight at the first signs of a storm."[44] Reagan, who by nature was inclined to seek a compromise between those advocating conflicting alternatives, chose to accept Shultz's advice. The president believed that the redeployment of the multinational forces would facilitate the creation "of a strong and central government" in Lebanon and would enable Shultz to implement a peace plan for the area.[45]

The U.S. Congress, in the meantime, although reluctant to challenge the decision of a president so revered by the American public, began to clamor for the removal of the U.S. Marines. But Reagan did not give in. On 8 October, in a radio speech from Camp David, he disclosed his stubbornness and total misunderstanding of the nature of the conflict in Lebanon. He emphasized that the United States could not stand by and watch the Middle East be incorporated into the Soviet bloc. Weinberger and the Joint Chiefs did not buy the president's argument. Ten days after Reagan's radio speech, at a National Security Council meeting, the secretary of defense called for a redeployment of the U.S. Marines to the ships offshore. He emphasized that, as deployed, the forces were "sitting on a bull's eye." Shultz responded by arguing that withdrawal would most likely incite the type of violence that had erupted when the Marines had been pulled out in 1982. Furthermore, he noted that the "policy was on the verge of success."[46] Reagan agreed with his secretary of state.

They were both wrong. Five days later, Reagan would experience "the saddest day of my presidency, perhaps the saddest day of my life."[47] He was awakened at 2:27 A.M. by his national security adviser, Robert C. McFarland, with the news that the Marines in Beirut had been attacked and that there had been "a substantial loss of life."[48]

Why did Reagan fail to heed the Pentagon's warning? His response can be attributed to a misconception and to his natural reluctance to consider any information that might question his belief on a particular course of action. Lebanon, in Reagan's mind, was vital to the national security interests of the United States. This attitude, however, was not universal. Pentagon officials, for instance, had for quite some time argued that Lebanon was of little importance to the United States. Even Robert McFarland, Reagan's national security adviser, had conceded that if "Lebanon disappeared, it wouldn't affect the United States' security interests very much."[49] Related to this mistake was the inclination of the president, his secretary of state, and his national security adviser to ignore information that indicated that the Marines in Lebanon were vulnerable to terrorist attacks. This information had been made available to the three decision makers by CIA and Pentagon officials.[50]

By February 1984, President Reagan realized that it was time to admit that the United States lacked the power to influence events in Lebanon, and ordered the removal of the Marines. The Lebanon fiasco was soon superseded by a new one. By the mid-1980s, the Iran-Iraq war had began to take on a new meaning among certain members of the Reagan administration. On 14 December 1983, Shultz and Weinberger urged nations to stop selling weapons to Iran, hoping that such an action would force its leaders to agree to a negotiated end to the war with Iraq. The rationale guiding the policy, known as *Operation Staunch*, was that the United States could not afford a protracted war or an Iranian victory. Either outcome, it was believed, would disrupt the flow of Persian Gulf oil.

For a while the policy had its intended effect. In the summer of 1984, the CIA was deluged with requests from Iranians and Iranian exiles for arms in exchange for information. McFarland, who since his days as an assistant to Alexander Haig at the State Department had been advocating the reevaluation of U.S. policy toward Iran, was impressed by this development and requested an interagency study of U.S. relations with Iran. The national security adviser believed that under the right circumstances fundamentalist Iran could be turned once again into a strategic barrier against Soviet influence in the region. He was supported by the director of the CIA, William Casey, who was convinced that unless the United States revived its influence in Iran, the latter would turn to the Soviet Union.[51]

On 15 July 1985, McFarland drafted a National Security Decision Directive that would have reversed Operation Staunch. This directive called for the United States and its allies and friends to "help Iran meet its important requirements so as to reduce the attractiveness of Soviet assistance and tradeoffs, while demonstrating the value of correct relations with the West."[52] Neither Shultz nor Weinberger supported the change in policy. The secretary of state did not believe that the power of the moderates in Iran had increased or that the Soviet Union could influence events in Iran better than the United States. More importantly, as he noted, the "proposal [NSDD] that we permit or encourage a flow of Western arms to Iran is contrary to our interest both in containing Khomeinism and in ending the excesses of the regime. We should not alter this aspect of our policy when groups with ties to Iran are holding U.S. hostages in Lebanon."[53] Weinberger, in turn, noted that providing weapons to Iran "would be seen as inexplicably inconsistent by those nations whom we have urged to refrain from such sales," and "would adversely affect our newly emerging relationship with Iraq."[54] This discussion, however, "took place out of sight and mind of Reagan."[55]

Much debate is still ensuing about when McFarland approached President Reagan with the idea of selling weapons to Iran.[56] It is known, however, that on 6 August, the national security adviser made his pitch for the arms sale to a group that included Reagan, Shultz, Weinberger, Vice President George Bush, and chief of staff Donald Regan. McFarland proposed the shipment of 100 TOW (tube-launched, optically tracked, wire-guided) antitank missiles in return for the release of four hostages. He also emphasized that such an action would help bring together the United States and Iran. Shultz and Weinberger reiterated their objections, and Reagan, after cautioning McFarland "to go slow," withheld his decision. However, several days later the president telephoned McFarland to approve the sale of TOW missiles or other military spares to Iran.[57]

The hope to free the American hostages in Lebanon and to block the Soviet influence in Iran by supplying arms to the latter suffered a major reversal in early November 1986. At that time, different sources began to reveal that Reagan had been doing what he had promised he would never do—bargaining with terrorists in an attempt to free American hostages. This attempt was not well-received by Washington's friends and allies in the Middle East. Although they did not welcome Saddam Hussein's drive to alter the power distribution in the Middle East, they feared more Iran's commitment to exporting its fundamentalist revolution.

Disclosure of Reagan's covert policy paved the way for a major reversal in U.S. foreign policy toward the Middle East. In 1986, Iran started to retaliate for Iraqi air attacks on its ships in the Gulf by using mines and small armed boats to hit neutral ships navigating towards Saudi Arabia and Kuwait. Kuwait, unable to protect its own tankers, asked the United States and the Soviet Union whether it could place its ships under their flags.[58] The Soviet Union agreed immediately, but not the United States.

The criticism caused by the disclosure that the Reagan administration had been trading arms for hostages brought the White House almost to a standstill. Led by a president ignorant of how to manage a decision making process, a chief of staff despised by Washington's power brokers, and a national security adviser whose days as the central foreign policy coordinator were numbered, the Reagan administration was in no position to respond effectively to opportunities and challenges as 1986 came to an end. This state of paralysis, however, did not last long. After becoming convinced that he could ill afford to be aided by a cast of advisers who had been completely discredited by their roles in the Iran-contra affair, Reagan agreed to name Frank Carlucci, who had served as deputy director of the CIA and deputy secretary of defense, to be his new national security adviser and Howard Baker, the retired senator from Tennessee, as his chief of staff. Carlucci, who assumed his new post in January 1987, brought Lt. Gen. Colin L. Powell as his deputy.

A sense of normalcy returned to the White House with the arrival of the new team. On 4 March, President Reagan spoke to the nation. He stated:

> A few months ago I told the American people I did not trade arms for hostages. My heart and best intentions still tell me that's true, but the facts and the evidence tell me it is not. As the Tower Board reported, what began as a strategic opening to Iran

deteriorated, in its implementation, into trading arms for hostages. This runs counter to my own beliefs, to administration policy, and to the original strategy we had in mind. There are reasons why it happened, but no excuses. It was a mistake.[59]

This acknowledgment set the ground for a new change in U.S. foreign policy in the Middle East. In May 1987, the Reagan administration finally agreed to Kuwait's request that some of its tankers be permitted to fly the U.S. flag. In addition, Washington sent several naval ships into or near the Gulf to escort tanker convoys to and from Kuwait.[60] Accompanying this policy was Washington's decision to return to its earlier stand of supporting Iraq in its war against Iran while publicly claiming absolute neutrality. This change in policy remained in place until the end of the war in 1988.

The year 1989 brought a new administration to Washington. Many of its principal protagonists, however, were not strangers to the city. The new president, George Bush, had served for eight years as vice president in the previous administration; the national security adviser, Brent Scowcroft, had served in the same capacity under Gerald Ford and worked on various presidential commissions (including the Tower Board); and the secretary of state, James A. Baker III, had worked as President Reagan's chief of staff and subsequently as secretary of the treasury. Later on, other veteran performers such as Dick Cheney, a Wyoming congressman and chief of staff under President Ford, and General Colin Powell, deputy national security adviser and national security adviser under President Reagan, were added to the cast—the former as secretary of defense, the latter as chairman of the Joint Chiefs of Staff.[61]

These decision makers did not share a common personality or a common belief structure. They concurred, however, on their perception of Saddam's intention. They all believed that the Iraqi leader was an ambitious man, driven by the desire to aggrandize his country's power and willing to cross another country's frontiers if such an act would serve his interests. But they also perceived him to be a shrewd politician capable of conducting rational calculations. To understand why these decision makers were surprised by Iraq's decision to invade Kuwait one must ask: Why did they decide not to implement a policy of deterrence against Iraq?

To initiate a policy of deterrence the creator must first believe that a viable threat exists. When concerned but not entirely certain about a potential adversary's intention, the potential deterrer can signal in the clearest possible way his unwillingness to tolerate any change in the status quo. In some instances, the deterring party must express its determination to use force if its warning is not respected. A policy of deterrence, however, can also carry some significant costs. If implemented against a party with whom the deterring party had been hoping to improve its relationship, it could well mark the end of the desired rapprochement.

For some time, Scowcroft and other top level foreign policy officials in Washington had hoped that the United States and Iraq would be able to resolve some of their differences amicably. The Bush administration had been encouraged by its success and that of its predecessor in creating a more cordial atmosphere between Baghdad and Washington. Warning Saddam that the United States would not sit still if Iraq invaded Kuwait could have foiled the entire process.

Foreign policy makers do not always have the luxury or freedom to complete their plans. It could be said that although Washington had attempted to cultivate a better relationship with Baghdad, Saddam's actions vis-a-vis Kuwait justified altering the original plan. Such a change, however, would have come about only if Washington had concluded that Saddam intended to invade Kuwait. But that was not the conclusion reached by the Bush administration. Scowcroft and many of his colleagues were convinced that it would be "irrational" for Saddam to initiate a new war after having paid such a high price during the Iran-Iraq war.

Why did the Bush administration conclude that Saddam would consider another war too costly? From the beginning, its principal members assumed that Saddam would assess the benefits and costs of an invasion in a manner similar to their own. They never accounted for the possibility, even as the information they processed gained clarity, that the Iraqi leader might eye the international environment through a set of lenses quite different from theirs.[62] They were so committed to developing a better relationship with Baghdad and so convinced that Saddam would recognize the folly of invading Kuwait that they placed little value on the tactical evidence that challenged their preconception. In addition, they engaged in what earlier was referred to as the *assumption of a single outcome calculation*.[63] Scowcroft and his colleagues, as they realized that competing inferences could be made from Saddam's deployment of Iraqi troops just three miles off Kuwait's border, sought to avoid the uncertainty of the situation by relying on categorical instead of probable judgment. In other words, Washington's foreign policy elite relied on a single, well-defined structure to construe an unverified situation in order to maintain its beliefs, feelings, and cognitions mutually consistent.

A leader's estimation of the costs he thinks he will accrue as he invades another country is in part a function of the obstacles he believes he must surmount and of the capabilities he thinks he can rely on to attain his objective, and not of the costs he incurred during a previous war against a country with different capabilities. Bush's principal advisers never took into consideration this simple dictum. Accustomed to making decisions in terms of analogies, they assumed that Saddam would weigh the lessons taught by the Iran-Iraq war and conclude that he could not afford to engage in a new war.[64]

There were three problems with these assumptions. First, although it seems reasonable to surmise that the Iran-Iraq war would had taught Saddam some critical lessons, Washington had no way of knowing whether the war actually had influenced his thinking process as he prepared to move against Kuwait. Second, even if Washington were right in its assumption that the Iran-Iraq war influenced Saddam's thinking, it did not consider the possibility that he might have inferred other lessons. For instance, Saddam might have concluded from the Iran-Iraq war that the next time he went to war he should attack a much weaker adversary, and/or that the best time to go to war against such an opponent would be immediately after suffering a major reversal, to prevent other adversaries from thinking that his power was slipping. The Bush administration forgot that this was precisely the strategy it had adopted in the past, and that the Ford and Reagan administrations had done the same.[65] And third, Washington never realized that the lessons it believed Saddam should have inferred from the Iran-Iraq war did not fit the problem he faced in August 1990. Regardless of how costly it had been to Iraq and Saddam to be involved in an eight-year war with Iran, Kuwait's military capability was insignificant when compared to Iran's. The Iraq-Iran war analogy, in other words, did not apply to Kuwait.

Thus far this study has argued that the Bush administration did not implement a policy of deterrence because its principal foreign policy makers did not want to upset Washington's improving relationship with Baghdad, and because it assumed that Saddam would conclude that the invasion would be too costly. This general argument can be strengthened by focusing on Gen. Colin Powell's failure to recognize the conflict between two goals as he sought to evaluate Saddam's intention.

The goals that seem to have dominated Powell's thinking process in the days prior to Saddam's invasion of Kuwait were predicting Saddam's intention and ensuring that the United States not send troops to the Middle East for reasons of symbolism. Alarmed by Saddam's deployment of troops, Powell tried to understand what the Iraqi leader hoped to achieve. As he searched for clues he failed to note that his aversion to using force to deter Iraq from invading Kuwait was biasing his analysis. His aversion was linked to his fear that the administration would be entrapped in another costly quagmire if it acted without specifying what the United States's objectives were and how far it intended to go to realize them. Vietnam and Lebanon were still fresh in his mind.[66] For him, thus, the prevention of the use of the military to send a signal and the discovery of Saddam's intention were not related—he could seek each value independently of the other. But they were not independent, for had he concluded that Iraq was about to invade Kuwait, he would have had difficulty objecting to Washington voicing a military threat.

Conclusion

Not all surprises are avoidable, but the surprise of August 1990 was. It was avoidable because Saddam Hussein never sought to conceal his intention with maneuvers designed to deceive his target and its friends, and because Washington had sufficient information to infer that the Iraqi leader planned to invade Kuwait.[67]

Surprise is a common phenomenon, but it is not practiced indiscriminately. An international actor is more likely to resort to surprise if it must battle with an equal or more powerful adversary than if it must contend with a much weaker one.[68] Saddam recognized that his action would be monitored by the United States and other international actors and seems to have calculated that if he relied on surprise he not only would be castigated by the international community, but also would be sacrificing the future use of surprise when the occasion might genuinely justify its application. He did not rely on surprise to overtake Kuwait, because he knew his country had the power to achieve the objective at very little cost.

The Iraqi leader began to prepare for the operation at least as early as April 1990. One of his first steps was to ensure that Israel would commit itself not to attack Iraq. He needed this insurance so that he would be able to deploy his troops near the Kuwaiti border without fearing that exposure of Iraq's western flank might tempt Israel to launch its own attack. Prior to and after deploying his troops, he gave the United

States and its leaders several opportunities to deter him. Washington refused to listen.

The United States was surprised because the Bush administration, in its hope to continue improving its relationship with Saddam's regime, believed it could not afford to signal its willingness to use force against Iraq unless it was fully convinced that the latter intended to invade Kuwait.[69] The Bush administration, however, had great difficulty envisioning such a scenario, because it believed that Saddam was too astute not to realize how costly such a move would be to him and his country. Officials in Washington believed the Iraqi leader would conclude, just as they had, that it would be unwise for him to engage in another war. This assumption was so ingrained in the minds of the Bush administration's foreign policy makers that they were unable to assess rationally the information which could have challenged their preconception.

There was a second reason why the Bush administration was reluctant to send a major warning to Saddam Hussein. The sending of a strong, clear warning would have involved threatening to use U.S. forces. In light of the costly lessons learned in Vietnam and Beirut, Pentagon officials were opposed to any attempt to deploy military forces unless the objectives were narrow and were specified prior to their engagement. This commitment on the part of the military had a major unintended effect. Fear of another quagmire made it difficult for U.S. military leaders to recognize that their desire to protect their institution was undermining their obligation to give the president an unbiased assessment of Saddam's intention.

The intent of this chapter has not been to second-guess the Bush administration. It does not argue that deterrence would have succeeded. Instead, it proposes that because of their heavy reliance on analogical thinking and their need to maintain cognitive balance, the principal foreign policy makers in the Bush administration failed to question their own preconceptions about Saddam's intention and the value of trying to deter him. Such a failure indicates an inabiliy to approach an international problem rationally. These defects were not corrected as they prepared their response to Saddam's invasion of Kuwait.

Chapter Four

Power Over Rationality

It is fatal to enter any war without the will to win it.
                                            —Douglas MacArthur

Introduction

In the early nineteenth century, Karl von Clausewitz wrote: "War is the province of chance. In no other sphere of human activity must such a margin be left for this intruder. It increases the uncertainty of every circumstance and deranges the course of events."[1] Clausewitz's message was clear—war should never be initiated before its makers analyze carefully its potential consequences. Such an analysis does not erase uncertainty, but reduces it to a manageable level.

And yet, few of today's international leaders seem to care about this dictum. Instead, when unable to compel their opponents to acquiesce to their wills by regular political acts, leaders of the post-World War II era have too often chosen the path of violence. They have focused primarily on Clausewitz's better-known maxim; "War is a continuation of policy by other means. It is not merely another political act but a real political instrument."[2]

The absence of balance between rationality and the willingness to resort to force has not been unique to any particular type of regime. In the 1960s, the United States did not pause long enough to evaluate carefully the significance of testing its will against a presumably weaker North Vietnam.[3] In 1980, Saddam Hussein's appetite for more territory caused him to overlook the fact that his target, Iran, notwithstanding its internal troubles, remained a viable power. In 1982, Argentina landed in the Malvinas convinced that England would not use its military power to claim them back. In each instance, the costs to the aggressor were substantial. The United States is just now shedding the trauma of its Vietnam experience. The Iraqi leader may have been driven to invade Kuwait in the hope that it would help restore his lost prestige at home and in the Middle East.[4] And in Argentina, the military, after years of ruling with an iron fist, had to relinquish its power to a democratically elected government.

The absence of balance between the want to resort to violence and the need to be rational, however, is in some cases restored by the presence of superior strength and the commitment to use it. As Douglas MacArthur reminded the powerful, to give birth to victory an actor must have not only the material means but also the will to win.[6] It was this lesson that saved the United States in 1991; it was this lesson that compensated for the absence of rationality on the part of the Bush administration as it decided how to respond to Iraq's invasion of Kuwait.

Capturing the nature of the Bush administration's foreign policy-making process during the Gulf crisis requires understanding how its principal decision makers concluded that it would be in the interest of the United States to protect Saudi Arabia and free Kuwait, and to rely on violence, instead of containment, in order to attain the latter objective.

The Decision to Deter Iraq

A little over a decade ago, a distinguished scholar of foreign policy making noted that "a president's search for quality in his foreign policy decisions must be sensitive to the constraints of time and to the proper use of available policy making resources. In many instances the search for a higher-quality decision cannot and should not be prolonged insofar as the failure to make a timely decision may itself reduce the likelihood of achieving a successful outcome. Nor should the search for a higher-quality decision on one policy question be allowed to consume a disproportionate share of manpower, and the analytical and intelligence resources that must be available to attend to other urgent policy questions."[7] Along with these wise words of caution, the same scholar reminded foreign policy makers that "high-quality" decisions involve:

1. Gathering the information required to make an incisive and valid diagnosis of the problem.
2. Facilitating the consideration of all the major values and interests affected by the policy issue at hand.
3. Insuring the search for a relatively wide range of options and a reasonably thorough evaluation of the expected consequences along with the possible costs and risks of each alternative.
4. Analyzing the problems that might surface during the implementation of the options under consideration.
5. Maintaining receptivity to signs that chosen policies may not be fulfilling the intended objectives.[8]

How a problem is initially defined has a decisive effect on how it is treated. Ideally, different interpretations of a new problem are considered and reevaluated as new information becomes available. This was not the case in August 1991.

The first high-ranking official in the Bush administration to learn about the invasion was Secretary of Defense Cheney. Two hours and twenty minutes later, at 11:20 P.M. to be exact, the White House issued a statement condemning the invasion and demanding "the immediate and unconditional withdrawal of all Iraqi forces." President Bush also ordered the immediate freeze of Iraqi and Kuwaiti assets—the latter measure to ensure that the invaders would not have access to the estimated $100 billion in investments held abroad by Kuwaitis—and that every diplomatic step be taken to turn world opinion against Iraq.

On the second day of August, Bush and his senior advisers held a crucial meeting. The president promptly made it clear that the United States could not permit Saddam to control 20 percent of the world's oil reserves, much less 40 percent, which would happen if Iraqi troops were to control both Kuwait and Saudi Arabia. Of great concern to the president were Saddam's plans. "Would Saddam withhold Iraqi and Kuwaiti oil? Or would he try to flood the world market? What would be the impact on U.S. oil reserves?" Bush's determination to narrow the problem to questions about how Saddam's newly acquired power would affect the United States and the oil market paid off instantaneously—his advisers accepted it without attempting to propose alternative interpretations or to contend that other values were also at stake.[10] Powell was troubled by the absence of discussion about how the problem could be defined, but remained quiet, by telling himself that Bush had an advantage over them because of his oil background.

With a definition in place, the discussants focused on how the United States could prevent Saddam from selling Kuwaiti oil. They considered several options. Cheney and Richard G. Darman, the budget director, argued that, historically, economic embargoes had not worked. Powell, in turn, questioned the idea of bombing the pipelines that moved Iraq's oil across Turkey and Saudi Arabia, noting that they could be easily and quickly repaired. At this stage, Cheney pointed out a critical distinction. He emphasized that it was imperative to differentiate between protecting Saudi Arabia and expelling Iraq from Kuwait, and suggested that they focus on the first issue.

The meeting ended on an inconclusive note. After hearing from General Schwarzkopf that the United States could either launch punitive strikes against Iraqi targets in both Iraq and Kuwait or begin a massive operation designed to defend the Saudi peninsula, Bush and his advisers focused on the issue raised by Cheney. Darman, who believed that no attempt had been made to define the objectives, doubted that the United States could do anything to save Kuwait. Bush responded immediately by noting that the United States could not afford to "accept what happened in Kuwait just because it's too hard to do anything about it."[11] In turn, Powell, who feared nothing was being decided, asked: "Don't we just want to draw a firm line with Saudi Arabia?"[12]

On 3 August, at a new NSC gathering, Brent Scowcroft, who had agreed during a private discussion with Bush that the case for action should be made but that the proposal should not come from the President, began the meeting by stating: "We have got to examine what the long term interests are for this country and for the Middle East if the invasion and the taking of Kuwait became an accomplished fact. *We have to begin our deliberations with the fact that this is unacceptable.* Yes, it is hard to do much. There are lots of reasons why we can't do things but it's our job."[13] Scowcroft's opening statement and Bush's immediate endorsement had a strange, but not surprising effect. Rather than engaging in a careful examination of the United States's long-term interests in the Middle East and how the invasion affected them, as recommended in the national security adviser's first sentence, Bush's advisers agreed with the proposition that the situation was unacceptable. Subsequent discussions focused on economic sanctions and ways the United States and the United Nations could erect a wall around Saddam. In addition, after evaluating a CIA report that warned that Saddam was determined to turn his country into an Arab superpower and that his troops could easily overrun Saudi Arabia, Scowcroft argued that the United States had to be willing to use force to stop Iraq, had to make its message very clear, and had to use the CIA to try to topple Saddam covertly. Once again, no one questioned Scowcroft's plan of action, and Bush ordered the CIA to prepare a covert operation designed to destabilize Saddam's regime and, if possible, overthrow him.[14]

Bush's next meeting with his principal foreign policy and military advisers was at Camp David on 4 August. After listening to the latest intelligence report from CIA director William Webster, Cheney, Powell, and Schwarzkopf presented "Operation Plan 90-1002." The plan, originally drafted as a plan to fight Iran or the Soviet Union, was restructured as a plan to defend or repel an attack on Saudi Arabia, and to move north to Kuwait should Bush make such a decision in the future. The decision to present the plan, however, did not have a particularly tidy origin.

Cheney, a veteran of many political battles and attuned to political signals, was the first to take seriously Bush's request to be briefed on military options. Concerned that Powell and his colleagues at the JCS were opposed to presenting military alternatives before being told precisely what the objectives were, the secretary of defense decided to bypass the chain of command in order to gather ideas about how the United States could send a military message to Saddam. Cheney's apprehension was warranted. Powell and the JCS had made it clear that the Pentagon would not propose using force in a "surgical" and limited manner until Bush had decided what the United States would do as a nation; and such a decision, they emphasized, had not been made yet.

Events and the White House, however, soon overtook Powell's and the joint chiefs' objections. Immediately following the 3 August meeting, Prince Bandar met with Bush and Scowcroft at the White House, and later with Cheney and Powell at the Pentagon. Prior to the second reunion, Scowcroft called Cheney to inform him that Bush had ordered that Bandar be shown the plan the Pentagon had designed to protect Saudi Arabia and the top secret satellite photos that revealed Saddam's forces to be pointing toward Saudi Arabia.

Cheney had no difficulty accepting the order, but also knew that before meeting with Bandar he would have to make it clear to Powell that it was time for the Pentagon to present its military options, regardless of how unclear the objectives might seem. Upon learning about Scowcroft's call to Cheney, Powell recognized that his initial objection was no longer relevant. Bandar was given everything ordered by the president. Specifically, he was informed about Operation Plan 90-1002 and the number of troops that would be deployed in Saudi Arabia if King Fahd were to agree to Washington's plan.

The meeting on 4 August thus became a mere formality. After Powell finished presenting the rationale behind Operation Plan 90-1002, pointing out that it had both a "deterrence piece and a war-fighting piece," Schwarzkopf discussed the specifics of the operation. He noted that it would take seventeen weeks to implement fully the deterrence aspect of the plan and that it would entail deploying some two hundred thousand to two hundred fifty thousand Army, Air Force, Navy, and Marines personnel. He then added that complete preparation for the offensive side of the operation would take eight to twelve months. He also stated that although the United States would have to rely extensively on air power were the president to order the initiation of the second phase, it was imperative to be prepared to launch a ground attack also. Cheney and Powell emphasized that they did not want to rely solely on air power.

At this stage the discussion moved to the question of whether Washington should focus on liberating Kuwait or protecting Saudi Arabia. Powell, unhappy with the idea of engaging U.S. forces in an offensive war, made his point obliquely by noting that if Iraq were to be expelled from Kuwait, the United States would have to take additional measures to change the political and social conditions in the newly freed country. Scowcroft responded with the comment that Kuwait was "not popular among the Arabs," thus giving Bush the opportunity to state: "That's why our defense of Saudi Arabia has to be our focus."[15] The meeting continued with only the top officials present to decide how the United States would go about persuading Saudi Arabia to invite the United States to send its forces. It was concluded that Cheney would be the official responsible for presenting the plan to King Fahd, if and when the Saudi King agreed to see him.

As Cheney waited to find out whether the Saudi leader would receive him and his delegation, he continued his education on Iraq. From Lang, the DIA intelligence officer, the secretary of defense heard that the Iraqis "are tough as hell. They can go clear to Dhahran. Saddam is not bluffing." David G. Newton, a former U.S. ambassador to Iraq, told Cheney that Saddam relied on force, was cold-blooded, was indifferent to the suffering of others, believed he was tougher than the United States, and did not respect democracies. The ambassador wanted to ensure that his audience would not fall victim to its own "rational man syndrome." Two other experts substantiated Lang's and Newton's analyses, and emphasized that Saddam had one objective: augmenting his power.[16]

When Bush was finally informed that King Fahd would receive the secretary of defense, he told Cheney to persuade the Saudi leader to invite the United States to deploy its forces on Saudi territory.[17] Cheney and his entourage—which included Schwarzkopf; Robert Gates of the NSC; Wolfowitz; Cheney's press secretary, Pete Williams; the U.S. ambassador to Saudi Arabia, Charles W. Freeman, Jr.; and two lower ranking officials—arrived in Jiddah on 6 August. That evening the two parties met, and after listening to Cheney's and Schwarzkopf's presentations, King Fahd assented to Washington's plan. The secretary of defense immediately conveyed the news to the president. Bush, happy to hear that the Saudis had agreed to his proposal, ordered its immediate implementation. On 8 August, he appeared on national television. In his speech, Bush stated: "The mission of our forces is wholly defensive. Hopefully, they will not be needed long. They will not initiate hostilities, but they will defend themselves, the kingdom of Saudi Arabia and other friends in the Persian Gulf."[18]

The president's speech marks the end of the first phase of the decision-making process that ensued at the White House following Iraq's invasion of Kuwait. The issue to be addressed in the concluding pages of this section is not whether Bush could or should have opted for another policy, but how he decided that sending U.S. troops Saudi Arabia was the best policy.

The decision to deter Iraq was part of a process directed and dominated by the president and his national security adviser from its conception. The first meeting did not begin with Bush's asking his advisers to delineate their own interpretations of the situation in the Middle East. Instead, he took the initiative by emphasizing that it would be disastrous to the United States and the world economy if Saddam were to gain control of Kuwait's, and possibly Saudi Arabia's, oil production.[19] At the second meeting, Scowcroft, not wanting Bush to appear to be attempting to restrict the context within which the problem in the Middle East was addressed, took it upon himself to argue that it was impossible for the United States to tolerate Iraq's action. Ideally, Scowcroft's remark would have been interpreted as another perspective to be evaluated. But this was not the interpretation that resulted. Every participant recognized that Scowcroft was speaking for Bush and that the president was determined to do something that would show Iraq and the world that the United States had the power and will to act.

Saddam's decision to invade Kuwait had taken Bush by surprise. The president immediately concluded that the incident had altered markedly the balance of power in the Middle East, and he was determined not to accept any further changes in the status quo. Afraid that if Washington failed to protect Saudi Arabia, Saddam would view it as a sign of weakness on the part of the United States and, thus, as an open invitation to march into Saudi territory, the president decided that his only choice was to deploy U.S. forces on a large scale.[20]

Bush's approach to the problem in the Middle East was not the result of the type of process depicted by attribution theory. Bush did not follow "statistical rules of inference in interpreting evidence concerning various patterns of covariation to formulate causal explanations" about Saddam's behavior. He did not try to understand Saddam's action by gauging the degree to which his decision to invade Kuwait could be linked to one factor instead of another and by establishing how many other actors had resorted to invasion when faced with the same conditions faced by Iraq.[21] What is more, he did not engage in a similar process to evaluate the potential consequences of his decision to resort to force.

Instead, George Bush relied on the 1938 Munich debacle to infer that unchallenged tyrants view the absence of opposition to their attempts to aggrandize their powers as a weakness to be exploited.[22] It was not mere grandstanding that led Scowcroft to remark during a meeting that the United States did not "have the option to appear not to be acting" and later to add that although it would be hard to act against Iraq, ultimately "it's our job." Like Bush, he was determined not to try to appease Saddam for, as the Second World War had proven, the effect of appeasement on a tyrant was not the same as the one hoped. A tyrant, believed Scowcroft, responds only to pressure exercised with determination and great force. These lessons, Bush noted a few months later, lay at the core of Martin Gilbert's book, *The Second World War: A Complete History.*[23] Or, as he said on his 8 August speech, "Appeasement does not work. As was the case in the 1930s."[24]

Of great significance during the early stages of the decision-making process was the way Bush and his advisers perceived Saddam. Prior to Iraq's invasion of Kuwait, the typical perception was that of a power-hungry leader who would exploit every available opportunity to increase his strength, but whose experience in the 1980s against Iran had been so costly that it would restrain him from actually launching a major attack on Kuwait. They believed, in other words, that he was a "rational" calculator, one who never lost sight of the realities of power politics.

Many within the Bush administration had great difficulty in perceiving Saddam differently, even after he had proven them wrong by invading Kuwait. Bush, Scowcroft, and Powell, for instance, remained convinced for quite some time that the Iraqi leader would ultimately back off; they thought he would be rational enough to recognize that his country could not stand against the power of the United States.[25] This assumption, moreover, helped persuade Bush and Scowcroft that the United States would not be at great risk by deploying its forces on Saudi territory.

By ordering the deployment of U.S. forces, Bush automatically identified his two principal values: the well-being of Saudi Arabia and of the thousands of U.S. soldiers who would assume the responsibility for defending it. From the beginning he placed comparable weights on the two values but did not view them as being in conflict with one another. He believed that the protection of Saudi Arabia would not imperil the well-being of its early U.S. defenders because Saddam understood that it would not be in his interest to exploit the United States's initial vulnerability. In other words, Bush was aware that a premature Iraqi attack could inflict a high number of casualties among the newly arrived U.S. troops, and that if such scenario became a reality the Congress and the American public would accuse him and his administration of incompetency. He did not believe, however, that Saddam would order such an attack, because he was "rational."

Some analysts may be tempted to contend that, since Bush's decision to protect Saudi Arabia was not impaired by an attempt on his part to deny its potential linkage with the effect it could have on the lives of those U.S. soldiers responsible for conducting the task, the president was not afflicted by the malady typically associated with the search for cognitive consistency. Such a conclusion would be premature. To understand Bush's reasoning process it is necessary to comprehend how he and some of his associates inferred that Saddam would act "rationally" and would choose not to attack during the early phases of the deterrence operation.

To know one's adversary is one of the central tenets of good foreign policy making. From the beginning, Bush and Scowcroft assumed that they knew Saddam; their assumption, however, was baseless. They had not expected the Iraqi leader to invade Kuwait, because they were convinced that he was rational. Their error was in assuming that Saddam's definition of rationality concurred with their own. They never considered the possibility that Saddam could have ranked his values or approached risk taking in ways very different from those they had assumed he would. In other words, they did not take into account that although rationality is related to how values are ranked, the concept itself does not dictate the order in which they must be ranked. Furthermore, they did not consider that leaders of weak states, or states that have endured bad experiences but still have a great deal at stake, sometimes are willing to accept costs and risks which would be unacceptable to leaders of more powerful states or states that have been quite successful in their international endeavors.[26]

Bush's and Scowcroft's unwillingness to learn more about Saddam is also reflected in their response to the advice they received from Arab leaders. Upon recognizing that their Arab friends had been wrong in assuming that Saddam would not invade Kuwait, Bush had no qualms about letting them know that he had relied on their expertise. He did, for instance, jokingly admonish Prince Bandar for telling him that Saddam was "okay." But this acknowledgment was not followed by a renewed desire to know more about the Iraqi leader. Middle East experts were not asked to attend any of the main meetings to present their views about Saddam and to explain how he might respond to some of the options available to the United States. Dick Cheney, in fact, was one of the few high-ranking officials who felt that it would be of some value to hear what they had to say. Their advice came after the president had already decided that he would attempt to persuade King Fahd to authorize the deployment of U.S. troops to Saudi territory.

It is fair to say, therefore, that Bush's decision to deter Iraq, and his belief that Saddam would not attack during the early stages of the operation, did not result from an attempt on his part to understand the "real" nature of his adversary.[27] Instead, he relied on the analogy, that Saddam, like Hitler, was a tyrant, and that the only thing tyrants respect is power and its effective use. Bush's firm commitment to this analogy acted as a barrier to the search for information that could have jeopardized its validity. In other words, Bush not only reasoned analogically, but also relied on his analogy to keep his belief structure balanced. These two phenomena would surface a second time as he decided that the United States would have to liberate Kuwait.

The Decision to Go to War

On 30 October, the president met with the secretaries of state and defense, the national security adviser, and the chairman of the Joint Chiefs of Staff. Scowcroft began the meeting by noting that they were "at a 'Y' in the road," and could continue to deter-and-defend, or could begin to develop the capability necessary to attack. Powell, who was the next discussant, stated that if the president wanted to go the offensive route, the troops in the Middle East would have to be doubled. The chairman added that Schwarzkopf had requested such an increase and that he [Powell] supported it. Cheney concurred with the advice and went further. In his own mind, he noted, it was not a question of whether to go the offensive route; the president should want that option and should order its implementation immediately. Bush's response was succinct: "If that's what you need, we'll do it."[28] He gave his formal approval the following day.

It is normally argued that Bush favored doubling the forces in the Middle East over implementing a policy of containment because he feared that his administration would not be able to depend on the backing of its allies and the support of the American public for much longer. This argument does not tell the full story. The decision to expel Iraq from Kuwait, by force if necessary, was made by the president between 2 and 5 August, just a few days after Iraq had invaded Kuwait and some five-and-a-half months before he authorized the attack on Iraq and Iraqi troops.

On 2 August, as a National Security Council meeting on the new situation in the Middle East was coming to an end,

Bush, frustrated by his advisers' reluctance to take a tough stand, stated: ". . . we just can't accept what's happened in Kuwait just because it's too hard to do anything about it."[29] The following day, at another NSC meeting, he gave his full support to Scowcroft's statement that the United States could not and would not accept "the invasion of Kuwait" as "an accomplished fact." He reiterated his position on 4 August to the Kuwaiti emir, Sheikh Jabir al Ahmed al Sabah, by promising that the United States would help free his country and place him back in power.[30] And as if these statements were not enough to prove his resolve, he stated on 5 August, in front of microphones and cameras transmitting his words and image to almost every corner of the world: "I view very seriously our determination to reverse this [Iraq's] aggression. . . . This will not stand. This will not stand, this aggression against Kuwait."[31] As the world would learn a few months later, the president was not voicing an empty promise.

It is not necessary to present a detailed analysis of the decision-making process that ensued after Bush had decided to send troops to the Middle East to help protect Saudi Arabia; a description of some of its highlights, along with the ideas and concerns articulated by the president and his advisers, will suffice.

Near the end of August, the president's deterrence policy against Iraq received a significant boost. After days of personal and intensive diplomacy by Bush and Baker, the United Nations authorized the navies of the United States and other countries to use force against any ship attempting to trade with Iraq. This act, however, immediately created unintended expectations. Major foreign policy and political figures inside and outside the Bush administration believed that since the United States had the backing of the United Nations, the president should give containment time to undermine Saddam's power and resolve. One person who expressed this view was the former chairman of the Joint Chiefs of Staff, Admiral William J. Crowe, Jr. On 28 November, in testimony before the Senate Armed Services Committee chaired by Senator Sam Nunn, Crowe stated that the United States "should give sanctions a fair chance before we discard them. I personally believe they will bring him to his knees, ultimately, but I would be the first to admit, that is a speculative judgment. If, in fact, the sanctions will work in 12 to 18 months instead of six months, the trade-off of avoiding war with its attendant sacrifices and uncertainties would, in my estimation, be more than worth it." Crowe's testimony was backed by that of another retired JCS chairman, Gen. David C. Jones.[32]

Crowe and Jones's opinions differed little from those voiced in private by several members of the Bush administration. General Powell, for instance, had become convinced that the sanctions against Saddam's regime were working and that if the United States and its allies were willing to wait not weeks but months, ultimately they would trigger some type of response. Wolfowitz was less sure than Powell, but still believed that under the right conditions containment could succeed. In his own mind, the strategy of containment was defensible only if the United States and its allies were willing to implement it indefinitely. Saddam's adversaries could not afford to imply that they would implement containment for only one year or eighteen months, for that would give the Iraqi leader a justification for calling on his people to be patient and courageous. A third member of the Pentagon who favored containment was Lt. Gen. George Lee Butler. As head of Plans and Policy, he had outlined four options for the United States: 1) continue with the defense of Saudi Arabia; 2) implement containment for another six months to one year; 3) go to war; 4) increase the allied forces in order to signal Saddam that a war would ensue if he did not acquiesce. Butler favored the long-term implementation of containment over war. The fourth high-ranking Pentagon official who did not favor war was the person who ultimately would be responsible for leading the allied forces into battle, General Schwarzkopf. He acknowledged that wars were sometimes necessary, but feared that trying to liberate Kuwait would be messy and bloody.

The most important believer in containment in the Bush administration, however, turned out to be Secretary of State Baker. He had worked assiduously to persuade the United Nations to authorize the international blockade against Iraq, and had ordered the Department of State to develop an analysis explaining the advantages of containment. Also of great concern to Baker was the foundation on which the Gulf policy had been erected. He did not believe that the American public was terribly concerned about the plight of Kuwait or Iraq's control over vast amounts of oil. He believed that it would be in the interest of the Bush administration to shift the emphasis to the American hostages held by Saddam's forces in Iraq and Kuwait.[33]

The supporters of containment, however, were not willing to put their political prestige on the line by advocating a policy they knew the president did not favor. After Bush had ordered the deployment of U.S. forces to protect Saudi Arabia, many of his advisers began to suspect that he and Scowcroft were becoming more and more committed to using force to free Kuwait. Hoping to reverse this trend, Powell tried to convince Cheney that the president should give containment a chance. Powell was not speaking just for himself; he knew that he had the full backing of his colleagues at the JCS. The secretary of defense, however, was not persuaded by the chairman's argument. "I don't know," he answered. "I don't think the President will buy it."[34] According to Cheney, Bush could not afford to live with containment, because it would leave Kuwait under Iraq's control. He then added that tolerating the new status quo would constitute a failure to the administration, because in public the president had deemed it unacceptable.

Aware that he did not have an ally in Cheney, Powell decided to take his message directly to Scowcroft. During his meeting with the national security adviser, however, the chairman presented the case for containment without ever stating that he personally favored the alternative. Scowcroft's response was blunt. "The President," he stated, "is more and more convinced that sanctions are not going to work."[35] He then added that it was very unlikely that Bush would change his mind. Powell responded by stating that he just wanted to make sure that the alternative to war was fully considered.

In early October the chairman was given one more chance to stand for what he believed. Cheney, aware that Powell had been dissatisfied with how the decision-making process had been evolving at the White House, took him to a private meeting with the president. When Powell took the floor, he first noted that there were two ways the United States could force Saddam out of Kuwait: 1) prepare for an offensive option by increasing the troops in the region; or 2) containment. He then added that a case for containment or strangulation could be made. "This is an option that has merit. It will work some day. It may take a year, it may take two years, but it will work some day."[35] Without making it clear that containment was the policy he favored, the chairman concluded by asking: "Where do you want to go, Mr. President? As each week goes by, I am doing more. There are more and more troops going in." Bush did not have to think long where he wanted to go. He concluded the meeting by stating: "I don't think there is time politically for that strategy."[37]

Powell's behavior was typical of those in Bush's inner circle who believed that going to war should be delayed until containment had been given a fair chance. Whenever they spoke in front of Bush or Scowcroft they remarked that containment was an option worth considering, one that demanded patience; but they did not dare to stand up and be counted by saying: I favor this policy and I believe that it would be wrong to go to war without first giving containment the opportunity to achieve the effects we want.

Their reluctance to speak up is not an unusual phenomenon. Theodore Sorensen, who had worked closely with President John F. Kennedy, writes that "[e]ven the most distinguished and forthright adviser is usually reluctant to stand alone. If he fears his persistence in a meeting will earn him the disapprobation of his colleagues, a rebuff by the President...he may quickly seek the safety of greater numbers."[38] The danger depicted by Sorensen is particularly acute in groups in which there is a great deal of disparity in power and status between the leader and other group members.[39] In such instances, as Irving Janis explains, the negative effect of disparity in power and status can be overcome only if the group is led by a president who is cognizant of what he and his office symbolize and goes out of his way to ensure that he does not act as a barrier to the articulation of dissenting opinions.[40]

The foreign policy-making system designed by Bush and Scowcroft to address the Gulf crisis was deceiving. At first blush it gave the impression that both wanted other decision makers to feel free to express their views openly. This impression could have arisen from the fact that many of them knew each other well and treated each other in a very informal and friendly manner. As Bob Woodward notes, "[w]hen the principals met, Bush liked to keep everyone around the table smiling—jokes, camaraderie, the conviviality of old friends."[41] But the reality was much more complex. To begin with, a decision maker such as Baker, although cognizant of his high-standing in the decision-making structure knew that he could challenge the president only so far. He understood that his "inner circle" membership would be revoked if he did not ultimately acquiesce to the "dominant view."[42]

But this was not the only problem. Determined to minimize internal dissent, Bush and Scowcroft sought to create a rigid decision-making hierarchy. Colin Powell, for instance, came to accept that as Bush's principal military adviser he had a much smaller role than he had had as Reagan's national security adviser, and that Bush was very conscious of each adviser's status.[43] The rigidity of the decision-making structure was also reflected in how its principal figures approached the Gulf crisis. Prior to a major meeting, Bush and Scowcroft would discuss how they felt a problem should be defined and addressed.[44] Then, Scowcroft would begin the general discussion by advancing his interpretation of the situation and how it could be resolved. Since members of the supporting cast knew well that the national security adviser was speaking also for the president, they rarely dared to take a different stand.[45] Challenging the president would have meant undermining one's own political standing at the White House.

Why was the president so unwilling to give containment a chance? The decision to reject an alternative is not always linked to the belief that one's own policy would be more effective. In the case of Bush, however, it was. Bush had doubted from the beginning that containment would be enough to persuade Saddam to pull out of Kuwait. In his own mind, containment was part of a process; it was a necessary but not a sufficient step.[46] Containment was begun more than two months before the Pentagon had achieved the military strength it would need to protect Saudi Arabia from an Iraqi attack. Its implementation helped the Bush administration buy time as U.S. troops were moved to the Middle East to protect Saudi Arabia, and to signal to the world that the United States was willing to give Saddam the opportunity to come to his senses and recognize that his only choice was to pull his troops out of Kuwait. The value of containment, however, was limited. Bush reasoned that Saddam would not be persuaded by containment, for he would assume that if he waited long enough the allied forces would ultimately give up. It was not mere coincidence, therefore, that Bush ordered the doubling of U.S. troops in the Middle East just as the Pentagon was telling him that it had enough forces in Saudi Arabia to protect it from an Iraqi attack. At that moment, the president could have decided in favor of waiting until his administration had a better chance to decide whether containment would be enough to pressure Saddam out of Kuwait.

Bush's decision to opt for an offensive strategy instead of waiting to see whether containment would bend Saddam had its origin in the same analogy he had used to justify ordering the protection of Saudi Arabia. From the Munich debacle he had inferred that tyrants respect only those who have power and are willing to use it. The United States had shown its determination to use its power to protect Saudi Arabia, but that was not enough. Having attained its first objective, the

United States needed to prove that its resolve extended to the use of force to free Kuwait. Such an end could be achieved only by, first, increasing the number of U.S. forces in the region and, second, going to war if necessary. The first step would signal Saddam that his only choice was to pull out of Kuwait. The United States, however, had to be prepared to resort to violence just in case the Iraqi leader did not heed the warning.

The Munich analogy, although deeply ingrained in Bush's memory, did not dominate fully his thinking process. The president and his advisers, especially those who worked under the Pentagon's banner, were convinced that the United States could not afford to be dragged into another Vietnam-type quagmire. Powell's reluctance to send troops to the Middle East was always based on his fear that the military would be made once again the scapegoat for a poorly thought-out policy. When Powell realized that the president was serious about going to war, he made sure that if he received the order to attack, his troops would achieve the assigned objectives swiftly and at the lowest possible cost.

This belief was not Powell's alone. For quite some time, officials at the Pentagon had been arguing that the principal error of the United States in its war against the North Vietnamese and Vietcong was assuming that if it applied force gradually the enemy would be "inspired to sue for peace at an early level of escalation. . ." The war taught them that the other side took advantage of gradualism to build their own military and political capabilities. The lesson: if the United States had to fight a war with a Third World power, it had to use as much firepower as was necessary to quickly destroy the enemy's fighting capability and will.[47] This doctrine was verbalized by Gen. H. Norman Schwarzkopf in November 1990 when he stated: "If we go to war, I am going to use every single thing that is available to me to bring as much destruction to Iraqi forces as rapidly as I possibly can in the hopes of winning victory as soon as possible."[58]

Powell and Schwarzkopf had the full support of their civilian boss. Sometime in Novemeber, Cheney told Prince

Bandar: "The military is finished in this society, if we screw this up."[49] Cheney's days as Gerald Ford's chief of staff were not so distant that he had forgotten how difficult it had been for the military to rebuild its image in the years immediately after the end of the Vietnam war.

The Pentagon's determination to avert another Vietnam was shared by the president. Vietnam had taught him that if a president chose to go to war he had to be prepared to let the military make its own decisions and use the forces necessary to win it decisively and promptly. As he explained to a group of congressional leaders on 30 November: "We don't need another Vietnam War. World unity is there. No hands are going to be tied behind backs. This is not a Vietnam... I know whose backside's at stake and rightfully so. It will not be a long, drawnout mess. . ."[50] And he was right; it was not.

Conclusion

To question the absence of a rational decision-making process by an administration that brought its enemy to its knees decisively and in a very short time, may seem absurd—a practice attended to only by those who stand at the sidelines and have no voice on decisions of national significance. One can also add that such a challenge does not take into account that the severity of the situation in the Middle East pressed the Bush administration to respond rapidly. And finally, one can note that the Bush administration was fully aware that a war with Iraq, if not handled properly, could cause some twenty thousand U.S. casualties, including the death of seven thousand soldiers, the loss of approximately one hundred fifty U.S. planes over a thirty-day period, and the killing of two thousand Iraqi civilians.[51]

Although these counterchallenges seem reasonable, except for the first one, they fail to take into account that concern about the quality of the decision-making process within the Bush administration was voiced by many of its principal representatives. Colin Powell, who as leader of the JCS played a critical role in the planning and execution of the military operation against Iraq, concluded on 5 August, as he evaluated Bush's latest decisions, that the president had decided to commit U.S. troops to protect Saudi Arabia from a possible Iraqi attack without a clear statement of his goals or a document that laid out the alternatives or the decision. His concern did not diminish with the passage of time. Around mid-September he became particularly disturbed by the absence of a process that would enable Bush and his advisers to gauge carefully the costs and benefits of implementing containment for an indefinite period of time. The policy of containment was favored by many members of the U.S. Congress and military services, and by the secretary of state.[52]

James Baker, one of Bush's closest political allies and a very disciplined and organized negotiator and decision maker, felt that the president had decided to use the military to protect Saudi Arabia without asking his advisers what they thought about his choice, and that the level of force had been decided not by them but by Operation Plan 90-1002. Baker agreed with Bush that Saudi Arabia was important to the United States, but feared that the White House was in such a hurry to respond that it was not thinking through the policy's possible consequences. Of great concern to the secretary of state was the fact that during the early stages of the operation the first arrivals would not be able to protect themselves if Saddam decided to invade. As he noted: "These young men could be slaughtered if Saddam Hussein attacked."[53]

Anxiety about the nature of the White House's decision-making process remained strong as the weeks went by. On 30 October, just as Bush was getting ready to order that the number of U.S. troops in Saudi Arabia be doubled, Paul Wolfowitz, who as undersecretary of defense for policy had access to the war plans, was struck by the absence of a process of writing alternatives and implications so that the principal decision makers could analyze them.[54] This uneasiness surfaced once more on Christmas Eve, when President Bush, without requesting a thorough and careful analysis of the existing conditions, ordered the Pentagon to warn General Schwarzkopf to be prepared to launch an attack on Iraq shortly after 15 January, if Saddam Hussein's troops did not pull out of Kuwait.[55]

This case, more than many others, establishes that success does not prove rationality. The momentous decision of 17 January 1991, was not the outcome of a rational process or even a process similar to that depicted by attribution theory. The process was structured by a decision-making system designed to minimize dissent, and was delineated by a president's dependency on historical analogies to define problems and formulate policies, by his need to keep a cognitive balance between his perception of Saddam and his belief in the appropriateness of the Munich analogy, and by his confidence that the Iraqi leader would be defeated if the U.S. military was permitted to fight the war it had not been allowed to carry out in Vietnam.

This case also demonstrates, however, that neither Bush nor the military forgot MacArthur's advice, subsequently reinforced by the Vietnam war: "It is fatal to enter any war without the will to win it." The military, in particular, sought to ensure that the absence of a rational, decision-making process would be fully compensated by an unquestionable commitment to winning the war. This meant having the freedom to use the strategies and instruments necessary to achieve the assigned objectives. In other words, superior military power saved the Bush administration from absorbing the costs that often ensue when an organization opts for satisficing instead of maximization.[56] But is this a reasonable solution?

Chapter Five

Rationality and Power

Systemic and Decision Making Analyses

Students of international politics have been debating for quite some time whether it is preferable to study state behavior from the "inside-out" or from the "outside-in."[1] The first perspective places the source of behavior within the state—its domestic political and/or economic structure, or the personalities of its leaders and their decision-making procedures. The second approach attributes the cause of a state's behavior to the structure of the international system.[2] Thus far those who favor the "outside-in" approach seem to hold the upper hand. They agree with Waltz's contention that the large number of variables to be accounted for within the state precludes the development of a parsimonious theory. Furthermore, they note that "analyzing state behavior from 'inside-out' alone leads observers to ignore the context of action: the pressures exerted on all states by the competition among them."[3]

Neither argument holds true. Theorizing does not entail testing the relevance of a "confusing plethora of seemingly relevant facts."[4] Theorizing involves, in the words of Kenneth Waltz, creating a picture of a "bounded realm of activity." It calls for determining which factors are important and which ones are not, without "taking information as evidence and seeking more of it."[5] States can be differentiated by a number of factors, but this is not the same as saying that all such factors dictate the international behavior of states. It is the task of the theorist, therefore, to identify which factors are the determining causes, regardless of whether they are in the state or the structure of the international system.

The purpose of a theory is to explain and predict behavior. According to Kenneth Waltz, in the study of international relations it is imperative to differentiate between a theory of international politics and a theory of foreign policy.[6] A theory of international politics, such as balance-of-power theory, is

about the results produced by the uncoordinated actions of states. The theory makes assumptions about the interests and motives of states rather than explaining them. What it does explain are the constraints that confine all states. The clear perception of constraints provide many clues to the expected reactions of states, but by itself the theory cannot explain those reactions. . . . What will a state have to react to? Balance-of-power theory can give general and useful answers to that question. The theory explains why a certain similarity of behavior is expected from similarly situated states. The expected behavior is similar, not identical. To explain the expected differences in national responses, a theory would have to show how the different internal structures of states affect their external policies and actions.[7]

Waltz's distinction is helpful. The structure of the international system is important if one's intellectual objective is to explain the constraints faced by states and the reasons that, for instance, a bipolar system may be more stable than a multipolar one.[8] It can also help predict the general behavior of states that are almost equal in power at the top of the power structure. The theory, however, cannot explain why weaker states in the international system behave as they do, what causes the international system to change from a bipolar to a multipolar system and vice versa, why some states become more powerful and others lose power, and why states that dominate the structure of the international system do not always respond to its opportunities and constraints in the same way.

Until recently, most theories of foreign policy were designed to explain the foreign policies of different states in terms of their domestic characteristics. Certain foreign policy analysts, for example, have contended that democracies are less inclined to go to war than states with nondemocratic political structures, while others have argued that capitalist states, after reaching a certain level of development, tend to favor the implementation of imperialist policies. Kenneth Waltz has been critical of these theorists. He maintains that one of their central errors has been to predict outcomes from attributes. Democratic states may favor peaceful solutions to international problems more than nondemocratic states do, but this does not mean that states in the first category are always able to implement peaceful policies. As he notes, "[f]rom attributes one cannot predict outcomes if outcomes depend on the situations of the actors as well as on their attributes."[9]

Waltz's criticism is unjustified. Rarely have foreign policy theorists claimed that their arguments apply to every single instance.[10] Waltz contends that states with almost equal powers standing at the top of the international structure tend to respond to its pressures in similar ways, but that in some cases their reactions will differ significantly. Similarly, theorists who have posited that democratic states are more peaceful than nondemocratic states are quite aware that there have been major exceptions to their argument.[11] This qualification notwithstanding, foreign policy theorists must be better attuned to the need to incorporate into their argument exogenous variables.

This study acknowledges the presence of variables at different levels of analysis. It begins with the idea that foreign policies originate in the minds of decision makers who are rarely able to attain the level of rationality assumed or hoped for by Realists. Decision makers are the ones who interpret, correctly or incorrectly, the international system.[12] From a foreign policy-making perspective, international structures matter, but only in the eyes of those who must decide how to deal with them.[13] Realists, aware of this critical distinction, assume that international actors are rational egoists who are determined to protect and promote their state's national interests. Rational foreign policy makers, in other words, assess the opportunities afforded, and the obstacles imposed, by the international system and respond to them rationally by defining the state's interests and gauging its capabilities.

The solution is inadequate. Realists like to assume that in some cases reality projects itself loud and clear, with one singular voice. They maintain that on certain occasions the pressures posed by the international system leave little room for debate about their nature. When the political and territorial integrity of a state is threatened, its leaders recognize the threat and take measures to protect it.[14] This statement is based more on wishful thinking than on an analysis of the empirical evidence. Two examples will suffice to clarify the argument. Today, foreign policy makers find it easy to argue that appeasement does not work; but in the late 1930s, although there was ample evidence that Germany under Adolf Hitler was determined to regain its past power and glory, few actors in the international system were willing to resort to force to stop Germany's drive to alter the status quo. In the summer of 1990, few foreign policy makers in the United States and the Middle East took Iraq's military maneuvers seriously, although its forces were pointing directly at Kuwait.

International structures, regardless of how conclusive they may seem, are perceived by foreign policy makers with different beliefs and analytical capabilities. Foreign policy makers may be egoists, determined to advance the cause of their state; but they are not equally capable of acting rationally, nor are they egoists in the same way or to the same extent. Just as two foreign policy makers facing the same international conditions, with the same decision-making capabilities but with dissimilar beliefs and perceptions, could easily propose different foreign policies, so could two foreign policy makers with dissimilar decision-making capabilities but similar beliefs and perceptions.

To contend that what really matters in foreign policy making is how foreign policy makers perceive and respond to international structures is not to argue that domestic structures are irrelevant. Foreign policy makers, particularly in democratic states, are concerned not only about the obstacles they must cope with in the international system, but also about the domestic forces that could derail the implementation of their foreign policies. But domestic constraints, like international obstacles, can be perceived and responded to differently by foreign policy makers with dissimilar beliefs, perceptions, and/or decision-making capabilities. Jimmy Carter, for instance, moved into the White House unwilling to play Washington's political games. For this he paid dearly, and thus it would be quite inappropriate to analyze the foreign policies of his administration without taking into account the domestic forces that worked against his administration. But such forces can be accounted for by focusing on how President Carter and his advisers perceived them and miscalculated their true dimensions.

Politics is not about structures, but about how human beings struggle to exploit the opportunities generated and overcome the constraints imposed by structures. Structures at the domestic and international level have frustrated, and will continue to frustrate, the intentions of foreign policy makers. A peacemaker will not achieve peace, nor will a troublemaker win a war, if their estimates of the domestic and international conditions are wrong. But to focus on structures without attempting to explain how decision makers perceive them and rationalize their responses is to assume that individuals do not matter, that they lack the power and will to affect the course of history. It would mean, if one were to consider recent history, that the existing structure of the international system would have come into being regardless of Ronald Reagan's military policies throughout the first eight years of the 1980s, Mikhail Gorbachev's domestic and international policies since the mid-1980s, or Boris Yeltsin's boldness in challenging the makers of the August 1991 Soviet coup.

A Typology of Decision-Making Aptitudes Revisited

In an ideal world, the analyst would be able to postulate a theory that would explain the reasoning processes of a variety of foreign policy makers. Such an expectation is unrealistic. Decision makers are not impaired by the same cognitive needs and analytical inadequacies. This reality dictates that the analyst uncover first the impediments that affect a foreign policy maker's reasoning process and then apply the theory that helps relate them to his actions. The same theory may also explain the actions of other decision makers, but this only means that there is a correspondence between the theory in question and the sample of decision makers to which it was applied, and not that other theories are inferior.[15]

The typology proposed in this book's second chapter differentiated decision-making capabilities according to the postulates of three different cognitive theories. These theories were placed on an imaginary continuum, with complete rationality, symbolizing the ideal decision maker, located at one end. Close to complete rationality lies attribution theory. From this theory it was inferred that the foreign policy maker defines international problems, evaluates competing alternatives, and selects options based on a quasi-scientific analysis of the situation. The foreign policy maker elicits causal explanations by trying to ascertain the extent to which an effect can be associated with one set of potential causes instead of other sets, and how often the same or a similar effect was preceded by the identified set of potential causes. From schema theory, which stands farther away from complete rationality than attribution theory, it was deduced that during the foreign policy-making process the decision maker relies on sparse information haphazardly combined in terms of "matched" concepts stored in his memories to address international problems. And from cognitive consistency theory, which symbolizes the least "rational" of the cognitive processes, it was postulated that the decision maker's need to maintain cognitive consistency affects the manner in which he attempts to find solutions to international problems. This need pressures the decision maker to overlook or discard information that may perturb his cognitive balance and to disclaim interconnection between competing values.

This typology served as this book's guiding rod during the empirical analysis of the decisions by the Bush administration during the Gulf crisis. The analysis sought to establish where in the continuum the Bush administration belonged. Based on the analysis of the Bush administration's failure to predict Iraq's invasion of Kuwait, determination to ensure that Saudi Arabia would not experience Kuwait's fate, and decision to opt for war instead of containment in order to expel Iraq from Kuwait, this study concluded that its principal foreign policy makers reasoned analogically, and that their psychological attachment to certain historical analogies undermined their willingness to consider alternative perspectives or scenarios.

At first glance, this conclusion does not seem to fit in any of the frames suggested by the three theories. To begin with, it challenges any expectation that the Bush administration may have been hindered only by its decision makers' "quasi-scientific" skills. Moreover, it does not seem to fall within the confines of either schema or cognitive consistency theory. Still, the structure of its reasoning process seems to be captured nicely by combining aspects of the last two. As noted a moment earlier, the Bush administration time and again relied on analogies both to define problems and isolate solutions, and to maintain cognitive balance.[16] This combination, however, is not in conflict with cognitive consistency theory. The theory informs us that stereotyped interpretations of dramatic historical events tend to close the minds of decision makers to information or points of view that could foster cognitive disorder.[17] It seems to be the case, thus, that so long as decision makers do not rely on historical analogies to maintain cognitive balance, schema and cognitive consistency theory remain as independent theoretical entities; but when they do, then the former becomes a subset of the latter. It is fair to contend, thus, that the decision-making aptitude of the Bush administration during the Gulf crisis can be placed in the least "rational" category.

It is also significant that at first glimpse the empirical analysis seems to highlight the value of accounting for the structure of the small group that made the principal decisions. As noted in the previous chapter, Bush and Scowcroft created an environment in which officials with very high status did not dare to promote an unpopular policy for fear that they might be excluded from the group's inner circle. It was also argued that the group's structure was so hierarchical that those who were not members of the inner circle were reluctant to express their concerns openly.

But is it really necessary to account for the internal structure of Bush's decision-making group when the analysis already focuses on his reasoning process? If a leader announces his preference on a policy issue and the members of the group tend to accept his choice as if it were an equivalent to a norm group, are we not suggesting that the only leaders who need to be studied are those with the power to determine what norms will be adopted?[18] Although it is premature to conclude that it is unnecessary to combine as "independent variables" the reasoning processes of the leaders and the structures of the decision-making groups that advise them until more detailed empirical analyses are conducted, it does not seem entirely unreasonable to speculate that the former has a critical impact on the latter. A president who tolerates cognitive imbalances, demands information, evaluates a variety of options, and does not rely extensively on the explanatory value of some deeply rooted analogies will in all likelihood create a relatively formalistic advisory group and will demand that its members air their differences in an open and systematic manner.[19] It was not the rolling of the dice that led President Dwight Eisenhower to design a system to sharpen National Security Council discussion and make it more effective. He was a man who, when confronted with a problem, sought to keep himself detached and to rely on deductive clarity to explain its nature.[20]

So far this study has traveled a relatively narrow path. It has assumed, as many others before it have also, that the quality of a foreign policy-making process is a function primarily of the decision-making aptitudes of its foreign policy makers. It is now time to broaden such a path and to inquire whether in some instances the structure of the international system affects the quality of a foreign policy making-process.

The Costs of Invulnerability to a Liberal Democracy

Rationality in politics, as has been stated on numerous occasions, is difficult to attain. George Orwell knew this well. He warned that politics, more than any other field of human interaction, is less an instrument for expressing thought than a means for "preventing thought."[21] In earlier eras, however, Western philosophers advocated the idea that the political good depends on the ability of man to transcend his selfish passions and cognitive needs and to use reason as a guide for action. Reason, they claimed, helps man distance himself from himself in order to promote society's well-being. An aspect of this notion was altered with the revival of democracy and the inception of capitalism.

Democracy was not universally welcomed at its birth. Many Greek philosophers, including Aristotle, placed it in the class of the corrupted forms of *politeia*.[22] This judgment weighed heavily on the minds of many great thinkers until the eighteenth century. Conscious that man rarely exercises his energies in accordance with some rational purpose higher than his selfish needs, they favored political systems that would promote rational behavior. Democracy, they argued, did not bring out the best out of man; instead, it fomented factionalism and the subordination of issues to personal ambitions.

The emergence of the modern market society robbed man of the belief that he should use reason to reach beyond himself for the good of society. Adam Smith placed the orthodox conception on its head by contending that society is best served when a man's actions are motivated by reason and self-interest. The use of reason to advance one's own interests, maintained Smith, promotes individual effectiveness which, in turn, results in the creation of an efficient economic system.

With man focusing on his own needs rather than society's, it was not long before the concepts of freedom and equality became banners for the masses.[23] For man to be an effective entrepreneur he had to have as his guardian a political system with few coercive bonds and discriminatory laws. But as the nineteenth century began to take form, many began to fear that Smith's ideals would reveal themselves differently from the way he had hoped. Two forces had begun to clash.

Democratization encouraged the masses to demand that greater attention be paid to their wants. People from all walks of life started to form interest groups and parties to promote competing needs. Concurrently, technological advancements continued to force changes in the nature and structure of society's economic system. The "invisible hand" remained in place as the component responsible for guarding the system's effectiveness, but its power became increasingly dependent on the expertise of planners.

In an ideal world these two forces need not have clashed. An economic system protected by an invisible hand and aided by the technical know-how of experts would have been responsive to the needs of the interest groups that would affect, and be affected by, its performance. In turn, interest groups would have understood that it would have been against their interest to blindly pursue their own needs rather than to calculate how they could be balanced with those of others and the system. In other words, to achieve an optimum equilibrium, the various parties would have been guided by an understanding of each other's interests, empathy towards the needs of others, and the capacity to address their differences rationally.

Ideal worlds are not to be experienced by mere mortals. With the further democratization of political systems and the increased dependence on planned markets, understanding and empathy gave way to intolerance, while rationality became a rare commodity. For Karl Marx this outcome was part of a transition that would result in the further deterioration of capitalism and democracy. His theory could not envision two groups with contradictory and conflicting material interests being able to negotiate their differences, at least so long as they interacted under a capitalist superstructure. He was wrong.

Some social thinkers, with their eyes on the past, hoped to reclaim the tradition that viewed man as a rational entity inspired by his desire to serve not himself but society. But by then it was too late—the new concepts already had developed their own deep roots.[24] It was not too late, however, for the competing parties to regain a sense of proportion. Aware that the fates of democracy and capitalism were at stake, they averted the proletarian revolution by fashioning effective compromises.

Liberal democracies have been tested by time.[25] Although on occasion some gave way to nondemocratic structures, and others modified significantly their old political structures, their record of maintaining their democratic foundations has been impressive.[26] It is particularly impressive if one keeps in mind that not long ago the fate of liberal democracies in the international system was being questioned, while today, with Russia and other communist states having been reduced to the role of beggars, there is good reason to believe that new democracies will sprout throughout the international system.

To the suggestion that liberal democracies have fared well in the international arena one must add a crucial qualification. Historically, political thinkers have had little trust in the ability of democracies to function effectively in a competitive international system. In the words of the famous French observer of American politics, Alexis de Tocqueville, ". . . it is especially in the conduct of their foreign relations that democracies appear. . .decidedly inferior to other governments."[27] International politics demands secrecy, detailed negotiations, patience, and, at times, rapid action. Democracy, on the other hand, "can only with great difficulty regulate the details of an important undertaking, persevere in a fixed design, and work out its execution in spite of serious obstacles."[28]

Builders of democracies have generally assumed that since the interests of the people cannot be shielded from the effects of developments in the international arena, and that since such effects vary little from one person to another, there was no need to grant equal representation to their voices when formulating foreign policies.[29] Moreover, convinced that broad participation in the formulation of foreign policies would catapult the costs of agreeing on policies to dangerously high levels, most liberal democracies emphasized keeping such costs lower than those generated by the reduction of representation.[30] High decision-making costs result in inaction, which may be tolerable in some cases, but not when the sovereignty of a democracy is threatened by another international actor. As it has often been asked: Why would a democracy want to secure full representation in matters of foreign affairs if by doing so it would risk undermining its government's ability to protect the *demos* from foreign powers?

The centralization of the decision-making authority in matters of foreign affairs, however, has not helped democracies avert some of the pitfalls encountered by states with different domestic political structures. Specifically, liberal democracies have not always been effective guardians of their hegemonic status. Great Britain today is no longer the power that it used to be. And the United States may have voiced during the Gulf War its last hurrah as the world's hegemon.

The loss of power by these two world actors is often explained as part of a "natural" international political process. During its glory days, the international hegemon, conscious that other states are striving to augment their powers, seeks to ensure that none succeeds in replacing it at the top of the hierarchy. This commitment draws the hegemon to overextend militarily and economically. Its capability to manage and possibly enlarge the empire, however, begins to falter as the power of its rivals increases. Ultimately, the increasing costs of governing the empire pressure the hegemon to retrench.[31]

At first glance the argument seems theoretically sound. It helps explain the fate not only of liberal democracies but also of nondemocratic empires. Any powerful state that becomes a hegemon, regardless of its domestic political structure, is destined to descend someday from the apex of the international hierarchy.[32] And yet, there is an issue that remains a puzzle. The theory is erected on the assumption that the hegemon, like other international actors, conducts rational analyses of the conditions in the international arena and responds to them according to its calculations. But if rationality is not supposed to be affected by the conditions in the international system, then why is it that such a method fails to warn the hegemon against overextension, but proves to be quite effective when it must reestablish an "equilibrium between the costs and the benefits of the existing international system"?[33]

An international actor's need to be rational is in part a function of its level of vulnerability.[34] Economic theory informs us that when various firms compete, resources are usually allocated more efficiently than when a single firm rules the market. Moreover, as Oliver Williamson explains, the assumption of profit maximization may lead to accurate predictions of behavior where competition is vigorous, but the same assumption may not be valid for instances in which the conditions of competition are weak.[35] Although these two arguments have different subjects in mind, ultimately they can be linked by the contention that while competition promotes rationality, monopoly fosters the opposite.

Rationality is costly. It is costly for any firm to gather information, identify values and objectives, delineate and assess a range of alternatives, and decide which alternative to select. However, a firm interacting in a competitive market understands that, if it hopes to remain competitive and augment its profits, it does not have the type of freedom commanded by one that dominates the market fully to undercut procedural costs.

This argument can be modified to apply to actors competing in the international arena. While leaders of relatively invulnerable states—i.e. states that face little competition—have the luxury of refusing to look at problems rationally, their counterparts in vulnerable entities do not.[36] One of the paradoxes in this relationship is that although vulnerable states have a greater need than invulnerable states to be rational, they often lack the resources to be so.[37] As a first step one could propose that:

> *The greater an international actor's sense of invulnerability, the greater its reluctance to pay the procedural costs necessary to assess international problems rationally.*

To suggest that rationality is in part a function of vulnerability is not to contend that the greater the vulnerability, the greater the level of rationality. Vulnerability can elicit stress. A certain amount of stress can be productive, but too much stress can lead to low-quality decisions. It is known that in situations of high stress, decisionmakers tend to limit their search for information, evaluate fewer options, concern themselves with the short-term consequences of their alternatives, and rely heavily on stereotypical images of adversaries and on historical analogies.[38]

How quickly states become vulnerable is also very important. When states become highly vulnerable over a short period of time, their leaders are immediately afflicted by high stress and, as a result, find themselves overpowered by a series of nonrational psychological elements. It is paradoxical that the condition that creates the greatest dependency on rationality is the one that sets up the most formidable obstacles to rationality.

If an international actor must become vulnerable the most desirable setup is fostered by the slow increase in vulnerability. In such a case, leaders are spared the trauma prompted by intense stress and thus can begin to comprehend that in order for their states to remain competitive they must relearn to be rational. How swiftly and how well leaders regain their ability to approach problems somewhat rationally, however, is also dependent on how long they have been invulnerable. If they lead states that have been invulnerable for an extended period of time, they are likely to find it more difficult to regain their "rational" mode of reasoning than if they head entities that began to lose their invulnerability not long after they had attained it. In other words, socialization can reinforce patterns of behavior—the longer a group adheres to a style of problem-response, the more difficult it will find it to give it up.[39]

For some time now, students of international politics have contended that the United States is no longer the power that it used to be. Robert Gilpin, for instance, has noted that the "redistribution of economic and military power in the system to the disadvantage of the United States has meant that the costs to the United States of governing the system have increased relative to the economic capacity of the United States to support the international status quo."[40] The change within the structure of the international system has increased the United States' vulnerability in a number of areas.[41] In turn, the growth in vulnerability seems to have pressed the United States to analyze more carefully the connection between its interests and its resources and to respond more cautiously to international developments.[42] As Henry Kissinger noted in the late 1960s, no "country can act wisely simultaneously in every part of the globe at every moment of time"; thus, it became imperative for U.S. foreign policy makers to "relate the desirable to the possible."[43]

Kissinger's warning did not go unheard. Richard Nixon's successors seem to have responded to international problems more cautiously than their predecessors. But greater caution did not signify a new unwillingness to intervene in the affairs of other states. Instead, it meant that U.S. leaders would intervene only when they became convinced that the adversaries were much weaker than the United States.[44] Washington did very little to stop the Soviet Union in Afghanistan and never seriously considered sending U.S. forces to topple the Sandinista regime. In both instances, Washington recognized that its adversaries had the capability to exact heavy costs from the United States. Such concern, however, did not become part of the equation in 1983, when the Reagan administration was afforded the opportunity to topple Grenada's communist regime.

The Bush administration arrived in Washington unsure about the United States's level of vulnerability. Its principal foreign policy makers sensed that changes in Eastern Europe and the Soviet Union could benefit the United States, but few knew how to take advantage of the new opportunities. A common concern was that with so much new uncertainty in the international system, Washington had to think carefully before committing its resources.

But after a year in office, the Bush administration became less timid. During this time it concluded that Moscow was no longer the formidable international player that it used be, and learned that an easily won victory against an almost powerless adversary can help heighten one's image to a level high above that warranted by the event's actual relevance.[45] The Bush administration, thus, inaugurated the new decade with some of its foreign policy makers believing that the United States was now freer than it had been for quite some time to impose its will on certain regions of the world. One such region was the Middle East.

For decades, relations in the Middle East have been defined by a number of factors. Some of these factors have varied from time to time, while others have remained relatively constant. A factor that changed little, at least after the end of the Six-Day War in 1967, was the commitment on the part of the United States and the Soviet Union to ensure that neither would gain a significant advantage over the other in the region. An interdependence of vulnerability developed between the two powers. However, as the Soviet Union began to expose its internal weaknesses, this balance in vulnerability slowly gave way to an imbalance. One of the first leaders in the Middle East to understand the significance of this change was Saddam Hussein. In early 1990, at a meeting with President Hosni Mubarak of Egypt and King Hussein of Jordan, the Iraqi leader warned that without the Soviet Union as a reliable counterbalance, Washington would seek to become the hegemon in the region.[46]

As predicted by Saddam, the United States did not overlook the effect of the Soviet downfall on the Middle East.[47] George Bush and Brent Scowcroft exposed this awareness when they claimed in early August that the United States could not afford to tolerate Iraq's invasion of Kuwait. It is unlikely that either decision maker would have taken the same stand ten years earlier, when the prestige of the Soviet Union was markedly higher. But it was also this sense of independence that freed the two U.S. foreign policy makers from addressing Iraq's invasion of Kuwait rationally. Knowledge that the Soviets could do little but to ask that they be consulted exempted the president and his national security adviser from gathering the necessary information, defining the problem correctly, identifying the relevant historical analogies, evaluating the appropriate set of alternatives, and choosing the best policy. Invulnerability, in other words, afforded the Bush administration the opportunity not to worry about whether its policy was the result of a rational decision-making process.

A Balance between Rationality and Power

A theory of foreign policy making will not explain and predict the international actions of states so long as it is based on unrealistic assumptions about the mental capabilities of the foreign policy makers. To contend that a theory of foreign policy making must rely on realistic assumptions is to argue that its conceptual framework must be free of ideals, but not that the excluded ideals must be sacrificed. A good social science theory not only explains and predicts certain realities, but also proposes ways to improve them. In other words, it is imperative to ensure that the ideals sought are not the ideals assumed by the theory. Failure to discriminate between these two conditions impedes the analyst's ability to differentiate between that which is and that which is wanted.[48]

From the preceding empirical and theoretical analysis several lessons can be inferred about the types of conditions that may facilitate the formulation of well-thought-out foreign policies. Leaders of invulnerable states tend to disparage rationality. This tendency must always be held at bay by the recognition that even the mightiest are mortal and that their mortality is sought by many. For years the leaders of the Soviet Union believed that they could defy the odds, that they did not need to worry about balancing its aspirations as a superpower with its potential and actual capabilities. Today, as the twentieth century comes to a close, the Soviet Union is no longer an international actor.

Becoming cognizant that even the invulnerable can experience a change of fortune demands leaders capable of being aware of their own cognitive needs and deficiencies. The first step leaders must take is to keep in mind that they do not address international problems as they are, but as they imagine them to be, and that to the degree that their images of them are false, so will be their policies.[49] The second step leaders must take is to be aware that their images of and responses to problems are shaped by their beliefs. Leaders acquire beliefs about the environment in which they interact.

These beliefs help organize into relatively coherent structures an environment that otherwise would be terribly confusing.[50] The value placed on certain beliefs and the complexity of belief structures vary among leaders, as does the ability of leaders to deal with information that challenges their beliefs. Leaders seek cognitive consistency; but some seek it more than others. The greater the leaders' need to maintain cognitive consistency, the greater the likelihood that they will overlook or reject important information and that the state will experience costs that might have been avoided.

Third, some leaders must not forget that they tend to rely on historical analogies to address new problems. Whenever they are confronted by new situations, these leaders resort to analogical thinking by creating parallels between the new and the old. In the process, they envision experiences not as they are but in terms of simple relationships between a small number of concepts.[51]

It is doubtful that any leader, or for that matter any human being, could ever reason without ever relying on analogies. The human mind, although extremely sophisticated, is not equipped to process vast amounts of information and to conduct highly complex calculations. Analogies are used by most of us to simplify the analytical process. Too great a reliance on analogies, however, can give rise to two major costs.

As Robert Oppenheimer noted some years ago, the only way to learn that a mistake has been made is by making a mistake, and a mistake almost always comes in the form of an analogy.[52] A mistake comes in the form of an analogy because it tends "to obscure aspects of the present case that are different from the past one."[53] In addition, a historical analogy can function as a cognitive barrier. A strong belief in the analytical value of an event that has had a major impact on the international system will propel leaders to use it as an analogy, not only to define and respond to a new similar situation, but also to reject or disregard information or alternative analogies that could challenge its value. Leaders, thus, must always keep in mind that the greater their belief in the value of certain analogies, the greater the likelihood that they will rely on them uncritically to address new problems, use them to repudiate alternative interpretations and solutions to the same problems, opt for the wrong policies, and impose on their states unexpected costs.

And finally, leaders who have conquered much of their need for cognitive consistency and their tendency to appropriate historical analogies indiscriminately must be attuned to their naive ways of defining problems, inferring causes, and selecting policies. Leaders who are free of the first two types of constraints will be quite effective at discerning the attributes of other actors and social phenomena, inferring the causes of salient events, and predicting historical trends and the behavior of other international leaders. Their effectiveness, however, often will be impaired by their tendency to overlook the evidentiary value of nonoccurrences while making inferences about international leaders or situations.[54] Also, these leaders will frequently fail to account for their propensity to attribute "good" behavior by their adversaries to situational variables and "bad" behavior to dispositional variables.[55]

The actions by the Bush administration during and after the Gulf War alert us that the structure of the international system has become too complex for any democratic government to formulate foreign policies without carefully attending to the quality of the processes that elicit them. A democracy neither presupposes nor requires competency; if it did, it could not justify itself. But a democracy that hopes to affect the course of history cannot afford to respect this dictum fully; it must rely on the knowledge of experts and entrust itself to them.[56] This is the dilemma faced by the United States.

The actions of the United States, the leading power in the international system, affect the interests of its own people and of a wide variety of states and regimes on a broad set of issues. To become national leaders, U.S. politicians struggle to gain expertise in the game of politics. This expertise often serves them well both at home and abroad.[57] Gaining expertise in politics, however, does not guarantee competency on problems that are affected by politics but are highly technical in nature.[58] If the intent of the United States is to continue playing a leading role in the international arena, it cannot afford to be guided by individuals who are adept at analyzing technical issues but have a limited grasp of politics. It cannot afford to be guided by those who are politically competent and have a vision of what they hope to achieve, but lack the basic knowledge necessary to render judgments on technical issues, and are unwilling to question whether their perceptions of reality are compatible with reality. And it cannot be guided by those who are politically and technically talented, but do not possess the intellectual and emotional maturity necessary to recognize that some problems are too complex to be dealt with without the advice of experts.

Notes

Preface

1. See Thucydides 1982. For an excellent analysis of Thucydides's relevance to contemporary international relations theory, see Garst 1989.

2. Gomme 1962, 108.

3. See Tucker 1972: 4.

4. See Marx and Englels 1968.

5. Kuhn 1970: 11.

6. In 1971, Graham Allison risked the wrath of foreign policy analysts by analyzing Washington's and Moscow's decision-making processes with limited data. Almost two decades later we found that many of Allison's inferences about Moscow's decisions were wrong. Still, nobody today questions Allison's intellectual intent, and for good reason. His analysis, more than any other work in foreign policy making, showed the value of applying competing decision-making perspectives. See Allison 1971.

Chapter 1

1. This figure does not account for the 159 U.S. troops dead outside combat. It is estimated that altogether 244 allied troops were killed in action. No precise figures exist for Iraqi deaths. According to Department of Defense, U.S. Central Command, U.S. Intelligence Agency, and Greenpeace USA sources, Iraqi casualties

could include: 1) 70,000–115,000 soldiers killed before the cease-fire, 2) 2,500–3,000 civilians killed during the air war, and 3) 100,000–120,000 civilians dead after the cease-fire from civil unrest or war-related ailments. *Newsweek*, 20 January 1992: 18.

2. Rationality, according to Frank C. Zagare, can be equated with either procedural rationality or instrumental rationality. I will discuss in my next chapter the distinction between the two and will argue that the latter form cannot exist independent of the former, as it is generally claimed. See Zagare 1990: 239–42. See also Achen and Snidal 1989: 143–69. For the time being, however, whenever I use the term rationality, I mean *procedural rationality*. By procedural rationality I mean the process of gathering information, ranking values, considering all possible courses of action, carefully weighing the pros and cons of each of them, and seeking to maximize values.

3. See Morgenthau 1985: 5–8.

4. My challenge here should not be construed as an attempt to question the intellectual value of Morgenthau's overall work, but merely as criticism of his theoretical framework.

5. For an insightful reference to this problem, see Gilpin 1984. Contemporary rational deterrence theorists are likely to disagree with my contention that their theories, which can be said to be part of the Realist tradition, lack predictive power. I will clarify my argument in the next chapter.

6. Ibid.: 10.

7. See, for instance, for the Korean War, Paige 1968; for the Cuban fiasco, Vandenbroucke 1984 and Hybel 1990; for the Vietnam war, Walker 1977 and Berman 1982.

8. It is terribly unfair on my part to identify only the aforementioned scholars as the ones who succeeded in standing above the crowd. The works by Richard Snyder. H. W. Bruck, Burton Sapin, Margaret Hermann, Richard Hermann, Ole Holsti, Matthew Bonham, Michael Shapiro, Stephen G. Walker, and dozens of others played also very important roles. My only justification for isolating the four is that they, more than anybody else, were able to draw the attention of those who normally would pay little attention to nonrational foreign policy models. See George 1969; Steinbruner 1974; Axelrod 1976; and Jervis 1976.

9. See Hybel 1990; Schrodt 1986; Larson 1985; and Mefford 1985. I have purposely differentiated between those who seek to enhance the theoretical context and those who attend to the creation of more rigorous models. Mefford and Schrodt, for instance, although deeply concerned about the theoretical nature of their work, are best known for their creative work in model designs, while Larson and myself have been interested primarily in testing the explanatory value of competing theories. Needless to say, we hope that our works complement one another.

10. There is no question that the range of theories advanced in cognitive psychology is broader than the one just depicted. Attribution, cognitive consistency, and schema theories are just the most reputable and widely used.

11. I will depict the "ideal" rational process in chapter 2.

12. Two examples are Deborah Larson's study of the relation of Averell Harriman, Harry Truman, Dean Acheson, and James Byrnes to the development of cold war policies and my own analysis of the policies of seven U.S. administrations towards Latin America. See Larson 1985 and Hybel 1990.

13. George and Smoke 1974: 11.

14. Obviously, many of the affected parties in the Middle East, such as Kuwait, Saudi Arabia, and Egypt, also failed to predict the attack and, thus, must share the responsibility. None of these countries, however, had the United States's intelligence capabilities to monitor Iraq's activities.

15. See Waltz 1979: 123.

Chapter 2

1. See Bentham 1834 and Davidson 1916.

2. Morgenthau 1983: 5. Contemporary analysts still adhere to this assumption. They propose that states seek power—both the ability to influence others and the resources that can be used to exercise influence—by rationally calculating their interests in terms of power. See Keohane 1983: 508; de Mesquita 1981: 29-33.

3. For a more detailed discussion of this argument, see Bull 1977. See also Waltz 1979.

4. Bull 1977: 96–7.

5. For an extensive discussion of the intellectual nature of regime theory, see Krasner 1983.

6. See Keohane 1984.

7. For a general review of the state of the field in the 1970s, see Holsti 1976: 39–52.

8. See Keohane 1983.

9. Larson 1985.

10. For a more detailed explanation of this problem, see Hybel 1990: 303, note 2.

11. See Larson 1985: 24–25. I have adopted Larson's proposed research design in my analysis of U.S. intervention in the Caribbean Basin and Latin America. Although my principal intellectual objective in that research was to argue that between 1944 and 1983 U.S. foreign policy makers relied on analogies to define the problems caused by domestic changes in the Caribbean Basin and Latin America and to formulate their responses to such problems, I compared my conclusions with those inferred from the application of two other psychological theories: cognitive consistency theory and attribution theory. See Hybel 1990.

12. For an analysis of Eisenhower's decision-making style, see Ambrose 1984 and Greenstein 1982; for Reagan, see Cannon 1991. According to Cannon, Jim Jones, the chairman of the House Budget Committee in the 1980s and a congressman who had known presidents as far back as Eisenhower, believed that Reagan was the least analytical and most ill-informed president he had ever met.

13. See Achen and Snidal 1989: 164. The authors focus solely on "rational deterrence theory," and thus it might be unfair to challenge some of their conclusions. It is my assumption, however, that their notion of rationality also applies to Realism, as deterrence theory is one of its derivatives.

14. Zagare 1990: 239–40.

15. Needless to say, the problem becomes much more complex when the decision maker is expected to account for variability in

conditions and for the presence or absence of probability values. Let us look, for instance, at a football coach who, while preparing for a game, decides he has four offensive plays, faces an opponent with only three offensive formations, and can assign probability values to each of his adversary's defensive formations. Now compare him with one who does not know what probability values to assign to the same defensive postures. The first coach can rely on his knowledge of the various probabilities to *mentally calculate* what option he wants to use. (In time he will also have to account for learning on the part of his adversary.) The second coach, on the other hand, must decide whether he wants to maximize the maximum possible value (maximax), maximize the lowest possible value (maximin), minimize surprise (minirange), or minimize the maximum regret (minimax regret). He would most likely use the first strategy if his team is far behind in the fourth quarter and he wants to maximize his chances of winning, and the second alternative if he is ahead and wants to preserve his point margin. And so on. The point is that regardless of how much information either coach has, both must constantly engage in mental calculations. See Lave and March 1975: 138–43. Interestingly, Achen and Snidal use Steffi Graf as an example of a tennis player who may not conduct mental calculations when she plays, but may be assumed to do so. Lately, however, Steffi Graf has faced a series of defeats largely because, as one of her oppononets put it, she never develops a strategy before a game and other players have learned what to expect from her and exploit her weaknesses. I suspect Achen and Snidal would respond that their argument is validated by the second player's contention, because to beat Graf other players had to become "rational." But if that is the case, then what happened to Graf's rationality?

16. Achen and Snidal's interpretation of rationality parallels that posited by Kenneth Waltz, who contends that rationality among competitors ultimately means "that some do better than others–whether through intelligence, skill, hard work, or dumb luck" (Waltz 1979: 77). This type of definition would be inconceivable to anyone with a general understanding of the etymological anchorage of the concept.

By this I do not mean to suggest that the meaning of words ought never to be modified. I am merely contending that if changes must be made, the end result should not be, in Giovanni Sartori's words, the "proliferation of chaos." See Sartori 1975: 7–37.

17. Simon 1957.

18. Larson 1985: 35–36.

19. Nisbett et al. 1976: 101.

20. Stated differently, it means that the analyst will attempt to gauge how often an effect is preceded by one cause instead of another.

21. Kelley 1967: 194.

22. Nisbett and Ross 1980: 8–9; Larson 1985: 36. It is important to note that attribution theory is significantly more complex than the way it was just described. Lee Ross, for instance, proposes that attribution theory contends that the social analyst also attempts to conduct two additional tasks. First, as just explained, he seeks to attribute an effect to a cause or set of causes. Second, he tries to form inferences about the attributes, that is, about the dispositions of actors or properties of situations to which the same actors have responded. And third, the social observer attempts to form expectations and make predictions about the future actions and outcomes. See Ross 1977: 175. The two additional tasks, however, need not be addressed, as they do not alter the nature of the argument postulated here.

23. Larson 1985: 41.

24. A few words of caution are appropriate at this point. Careful consideration of the studies that come under the rubric of attribution theory show that some of their basic postulates contradict one another. Nisbett and Ross, for instance, propose that vivid information—information that is concrete, has an emotional effect on the individual, and is derived from personal experience or firsthand knowledge—has a disproportionate effect on the way individuals judge and derive explanations (1980: 43–45). Needless to say, this conclusion is inconsistent with Larson's contention that in attribution theory there are "no motivational constructs of any kind" (1985: 35). Furthermore, it challenges directly Kelley's thesis that in formulating causal explanations, individuals use information to gauge distinctiveness, consistency, and consensus. In using information for these three purposes, the individual is conducting an "analysis of variance" that resembles that used by trained social scientists (Kelley 1967: 194). The trained social

scientist, however, knows that he cannot permit 'vivid information' to have a special effect on his analysis. Nisbett and Ross's contention that this malfunction can be attributed to the analyst's lack of skill to conduct correct analysis fails to give appropriate weight to the strong possibility that information becomes 'vivid' because it affects some central values.

This long discourse has a purpose. Since attribution theory cannot assimilate both Kelley's thesis and some of Nisbett and Ross's findings, I have chosen to define the theory as presented by the former. This ought not to be construed as an attempt to question Nisbett and Ross's arguments and findings. The decision, instead, is derived from the assumption that if one is to construct a typology that depicts different levels of decision-making aptitudes, Kelley's model, with its emphasis on the decision maker's attempt to maintain an open mind as he searches for truth, comes closest to the ideal rational decision maker.

25. Cognitive consistency theory should not be confused with cognitive dissonance theory. The former assumes that the individual needs to develop simple rules for processing information in order to maintain consistency. It seeks to explain the process that takes place prior to, and just at, the time the decision is being made. The latter, on the other hand, with its focus on postdecision situations, is built on the assumption that ego-defensive motivations lead the individual to seek strong justification for his behavior, to the point that he will rearrange his beliefs so that they provide increase support for his action. See Jervis 1976: 38–3, note 2; and Lebow 1981: 111.

26. Quoted in Jervis 1976: 117.

27. See Steinbruner 1974.

28. Ibid. 1974: 90 and 111.

29. Abelson 1976: 33–45.

30. See Hybel 1990: ch. 6; and Lowenthal 1972.

31. One of the immediate effects of this process is to "obscure aspects of the present case that are different from the past one." See Jervis 1976: 220.

32. As I argue in *How Leaders Reason*, a first look at John F. Kennedy's decision to try to overthrow the Castro regime in 1961

could lead the analyst to conclude that the president engaged in a trade-off calculation between overthrowing the Castro regime and averting U.S. exposure, and concluded that a covert operation with minimal air involvement would be an effective way to fulfill both objectives. But I then contend that when the decision-making process is analyzed more carefully, it becomes evident that Kennedy committed the errors typically identified by cognitive consistency theory.

Kennedy committed two mistakes. His first error was to assume that the operation would not be exposed. This assumption did not correspond with the fact that in the Miami Cuban community it was common knowledge that an invasion was about to be launched, and that the *New York Times* had gotten hold of such information. Second, Kennedy failed to consider more carefully the possibilities that by reducing the air strike force and canceling the air support for the invading forces, he would be undermining the chances of the operation's success, and that if the invasion failed he would be augmenting markedly the likelihood of exposure. One might also add that Kennedy and his advisers were fully aware that Castro's military power had increased significantly since he had toppled the Batista regime. Former secretary of state Dean Acheson had warned the president that "it was not necessary to call in Price Waterhouse [the prominent accounting firm] to discover that fifteen hundred Cubans weren't as good twenty-five thousand Cubans."

Cognitive consistency theory emphasizes that in conditions of high risk, a decision maker who has doubts about the availability of additional alternatives will alleviate stress by ignoring information that would point to the risk. It also notes that a decision maker faced with a problem involving conflicting values will separate them, deny that any connection exists between them, and make a choice in terms of one value alone without estimating how other values might be affected. Kennedy ignored critical information and did not study the potential conflict between various values and his decision to authorize the invasion and reduce the air support. See Hybel 1990: 162–4.

33. See Janis 1972.

34. See Janis and Mann 1977.

35. Janis 1972: 9.

36. George 1980: 139.

37. It is very unlikely that a president whose behavior can be explicated by cognitive consistency theory will rely on the advice of an open and highly systematic decision-making group. It is interesting to note that John F. Kennedy's cognitive behavior in 1961, prior to the Bay of Pigs fiasco, reflected the tendencies typically associated with cognitive consistency theory, and that his decision-making group reflected the symptoms normally linked to groupthink. By 1962, however, Kennedy's reasoning process had become significantly more systematic, and so had that of the group that tackled the Cuban missile problem. See Janis 1972 for an analysis of the two cases; and Vandenbroucke 1984 and Hybel 1990 for explanations of the Bay of Pigs fiasco.

Chapter 3

1. A great deal of the empirical evidence used in this chapter and the next is taken directly from Woodward's new book *The Commanders* (1991). To avoid unnecessary references, I refer to his book only in those instances in which I borrow a direct quote. All other references, regardless of their form, are given full credit.

2. Quoted in Bulloch and Morris 1991: 100.

3. At this meeting, Saddam did not mention any Arab country by name. According to Walid Khalidi, however, six weeks later Iraq's foreign minister, Tariq Aziz, in a thirty-seven page memorandum dated 15 July 1990, explicitly named Kuwait and the United Arab Emirates as the two culprits in overproduction. Aziz also claimed that between 1980 and 1990 Kuwait had pumped $2.4 billion worth of oil belonging to Iraq from Rumaileh, a field shared by the two countries. See Khalidi 1991: 57-65.

4. The movement of troops, however, is unlikely to have been the only new major signal evaluated by the Department of Defense analyst. On 16 July, Iraq had sent a letter to the secretary-general of the Arab League detailing its grievances against Kuwait and the United Arab Emirates. Furthermore, on 17 July in his Revolution Day speech, Saddam launched a ferocious verbal attack against the two countries, contending that both were acting as agents of the imperialist powers. See *The Economist* 1991: 104.

5. I will discuss the assessment in greater detail in a later section. For the time being it is sufficient to know that Israeli and U.S. intelligence analysts and foreign policy makers had become convinced that Iraq's war with Iran had made Saddam a "chastened man, aware of the limits of Iraq's power and eager to bind his country to the West." *The Economist* 1991: 101

6. I will discuss aspects of this meeting in a later section.

7. Some of these leaders seem to have been encouraged by Iraq's behavior during the OPEC meeting held in Geneva during the last week of July 1990. At the beginning of the meeting, Iraq demanded a $25 a barrel benchmark price to replace the current $18. Saudi Arabia opposed such a high price, and ultimately OPEC members compromised on a $21 price. Iraq left the meeting without expressing strong resentment about its inability to get what it had demanded. It is important to keep in mind, however, that Iraq continued to move troops to its borders with Kuwait. See Bulloch and Morris 1991: 102–3.

8. Quoted in Woodward, 1991: 216–7.

9. It may be useful to keep in mind that by this time some nongovernmental organizations, with significantly more limited resources, were wondering whether Saddam might be preparing to launch an attack. *The Economist*, for instance, wrote on 21 July 1990, less than two weeks before the attack, that the latest steps taken by Iraq sounded "alarmingly like a pretext for invasion." See *The Economist* 1991: 104.

10. Stein 1982: 95.

11. Hybel 1986: 9

12. Whaley 1973: 139.

13. Hybel 1986: 13–4.

14. Quoted in *The Economist* 1991: 100.

15. Ibid.: 102.

16. Quoted in Woodward 1991: 201.

17. See Bulloch and Morris 1991: 101.

18. See Seaton 1971: 9 and Langer and Cleason 1953: 14.

19. I am not suggesting that Saddam borrowed his strategy from Hitler, but I would not be surprised if he did. For the moment, however, I am merely proposing that the two strategies were similar.

20. Bandar arrived at the same conclusion in early August, shortly after Iraq had invaded Kuwait. "Saddam," he thought, "had sought and received American and Israeli assurances he would not be attacked. He had protected his western flank with Israel, freeing him to do what he wanted on the east with Kuwait." Woodward 1991: 239.

21. Walter Lang and CIA analysts were initially perplexed by this move. They could not understand why Saddam would redeploy his forces to the west and risk an Israeli attack. This lack of understanding seems to indicate that these analysts were unaware that Iraq had been reassured by the Bush administration that Israel had no intention of attacking it.

22. Quoted in Woodward 1991: 219.

23. George and Smoke 1974: 582.

24. Knorr 1964: 459.

25. Hybel 1986: 15–6.

26. Ibid.: 17. A case that supports this argument was Japan's decision not to try to disguise its intention to go to war in 1941. Japan knew that it would not be able to conceal the preparations that preceded the launching of the attacks throughout Southeast Asia. Its principal strategy was to conceal its real capabilities along with one of its targets: Pearl Harbor. See Hybel 1986: 26.

27. Quoted in Woodward 1991: 210.

28. Emphasis added. All the quotes and interpretations come directly from the transcript of the meeting, as released by Baghdad. See *The Glaspie Transcript* 1991: 122–133.

29. She was particularly critical of Diane Sawyer's program on ABC. "What happened in the program," she said to Saddam, "was cheap and unjust. And this is the real picture of what happens in the American media—even to American politicians themselves." See *The Glaspie Transcript* 1991: 129.

30. This passage reinforces our previous contention that the United States had been monitoring closely Saddam's and his foreign minister's earlier speeches and letters.

31. Ambassador Glaspie may have believed that she was conveying the United States's great concern when she asked Saddam Hussein to explain what his intentions were. The problem is that she never really made it clear that the United States would not tolerate an aggressive act on the part of Iraq. To begin with, she began her question by noting that her government "did not have an opinion on the Arab-Arab conflicts, like [Iraq's] border disagreement with Kuwait." And then, after having posed the question, rather than attempting to emphasize how difficult it would be for the United States to tolerate an Iraqi invasion, she stated: "I simply describe the concern of my government." See *The Glaspie Transcript* 1991: 130.

32. Quoted in Khadduri 1988: 142–43. See also Brzezinski 1983: 443.

33. Brzezinski 1983: 444.

34. Khadduri 1988: 143–44.

35. Bulloch and Morris 1989: 142.

36. Sick 1989: 131. Truman, however, was not the first U.S. president to assume that U.S. interests could be affected by developments in the Middle East. In 1943, President Franklin D. Roosevelt declared: "The defense of Saudi Arabia is vital to the defense of the United States." Quoted in Stork and Wenger 1991: 34.

37. Khadduri 1988: 144–45.

38. For a detailed and excellent account of how the Reagan administration responded to the war in Lebanon, see Cannon 1991: 389–457.

39. Quoted in Haig 1984: 337.

40. Quoted in Martin and Walcott 1988: 93.

41. See Cannon 1991: 398–99. By this time George Shultz had already been asked by Reagan to replace Haig as secretary of state. Haig, however, remained in his post until 5 July. Reagan's decision was not made public until 6 July.

42. Cannon 1991: 405–6. Powell, as we shall see, had similar misgivings about sending U.S. troops abroad. Regarding Lebanon, he noted that sending troops to Beirut "wasn't sensible and never did serve a purpose. It was goofy from the beginning." Lebanon became an experience the general would not forget easily.

43. Ibid.: 416.

44. Ibid.: 406 and 418.

45. Ibid.: 409.

46. Ibid.: 439.

47. Reagan 1990: 437.

48. Cannon 1991: 442. Two hundred and forty one U.S. Marines died in the attack. The French contingent lost fifty eight of its paratroopers during an attack at approximately the same time, two miles away from the U.S. Marines headquarters.

49. Ibid.: 449.

50. Ibid.: 443.

51. Ibid.: 600–3.

52. Ibid.: 604.

53. Report of the President's Special Review Board (Tower Report) 1987: B–4.

54. Weinberger 1990: 363–64.

55. Cannon 1991: 605.

56. For an excellent attempt to shed some light on the Iran-Contra controversy, see Cannon 1991: chaps. 19 and 20.

57. The actual deal involved Israel's selling the TOWs to Iran, with the United States then replenishing the stock of Israeli weapons.

58. For an account of Kuwait's diplomatic maneuvers during this period, see Draper 1991: 40–56.

59. Address to the nation on the Iran arms and Contra aid controversy, 4 March 1987.

60. Sick 1989: 132.

61. Robert Gates was appointed deputy to Scowcroft. Gates had served under President Reagan as deputy director of the CIA, and had been nominated to head the same agency after its director William Casey died, but withdrew his name to avert possible rejection by the Senate due to CIA involvement in the Iran-Contra affair.

62. See Jervis 1976: 145.

63. See chapter 2, particularly the discussion on cognitive consistency theory.

64. The contention that the Bush administration thought in terms of analogies was reaffirmed by a former member of its National Security Council, Dr. Condoleezza Rice, at a public seminar at the University of Southern California in April 1991.

65. I am referring to the handling of the Mayaguez incident and the Angola war by the Ford administration; Grenada and Libya by the Reagan administration; and Panama by the Bush administration.

66. Woodward 1991: 215–16.

67. Shortly after Iraq had invaded Kuwait, Saddam noted that he had provided adequate warning of his intentions during the ten weeks prior to the invasion. See Bulloch and Morris 1991: 105.

68. See Hybel 1986.

69. It is now evident that top officials in the Bush administration tried to bring Saddam Hussein "into the family of nations" (Bush's own words) through economic and political means, and that the Iraqi leader used the economic assistance to further develop his military arsenal. *New York Times*, 24 June 1992:A7.

Chapter 4

1. Clausewitz 1990: 295.

2. Ibid.: 298.

3. The Soviet Union committed the same error in regard to Afghanistan in 1980.

4. Obviously one must also take into account the terrible effect of the Iraq-Iran war on Iraq's economy.

5. In the case of Argentina, although the war brought high costs to both the military and the civilian population, ultimately it was a blessing in disguise for the latter. I will analyze in greater detail. in the last chapter, the relationship between rationality and power. Specifically, I will explain the effect an international actor's standing in the structure of the international system has on its foreign policy-making process.

6. Please refer to the quote at the beginning of this chapter.

7. George 1980: 1–2.

8. Ibid.: 10.

9. These questions were attributed by Woodward to Bush, but were not presented in the text as direct quotes. See Woodward 1991: 226. Theodore Draper, in an article critical of U.S. oil policy in the Middle East in 1987, asserts that at that time the American public was fed dubious statistical propaganda about the indispensability of Gulf oil. He quotes experts such as Mazher Hameed and S. Fred Singer, who have contended that the United States and the industrialized world were not terribly dependent on Kuwaiti oil. Based on their arguments, Draper concludes that the United States should have not aided Kuwait when its leaders asked Washington for their oil tankers be protected. Draper's argument, however, does not apply fully to the situation in 1990, for both experts exclude Saudi Arabia from the equation. Hameed, for instance, states: "A cut-off of Gulf oil that did not include Saudi production would be ineffective, because, due to the enormous Saudi production capacity, the country alone could match most current Gulf petroleum exports." Hameed's argument, in fact, reinforces Bush's belief that it was imperative for the United States to protect Saudi Arabia. The argument, however, does question Bush's contention that the United States could not afford to lose Kuwait to Iraq. See Draper 1991: 50–51.

An alternative argument, and possibly a more effective one, is postulated by Thomas L. Friedman. According to this writer, Iraq's control of 40 percent of the world's oil reserve would not necessarily lead its leaders to increase its price to unreasonable levels. The Iraqis, notes Friedman, "understand the world oil market as well as the Saudis. That means understanding that if prices are pushed too high too fast, the West will find alternative energy sources, which will sooner or later drive the price of oil way down." See Friedman 1991: 205.

For our purposes it is not important whose argument is correct—Bush's, Hameed's, or Friedman's. What is critical is that no single member within the Bush administration dared to challenge Bush with arguments similar to those proposed by either Hameed or Friedman.

10. Elizabeth Drew, the Washington correspondent of *The New Yorker* presents a somewhat different argument. She contends that from the moment Iraq invaded Kuwait, the Bush administration viewed the act as a threat to U.S. oil interests in the Gulf and as a menace to other Arab states and Israel. She also maintains that these same decision makers feared that Saddam, if not stopped, would eventually try to use chemical or nuclear weapons against Israel. She concludes by contending that from almost the beginning "the United States was committed to reducing Iraq's military strength irrespective of Kuwait." Drew 1991: 182.

I have no way of ascertaining Drew's argument. However, it seems quite strange that Woodward, who seems to have had very good access to those who participated in the decision-making process during that first meeting, never mentions Israel and the fear that Saddam might some day try to use nuclear or chemical weapons against its population. I also suspect that the Bush administration knew that Israeli leaders had been monitoring very closely developments in Iraq and would have taken whatever measures they deemed appropriate to stop Iraq if they suspected it was planning to use its nuclear and chemical arsenal against Israel.

11. Ibid.: 229.

12. Ibid.

13. Ibid.: 237. My emphasis. It is important to repeat that, as far as one can gather from Woodward's account, the threat Iraq could pose to Israel had not been discussed yet by members of the Bush administration. It is not difficult to understand why. Although the Bush administration was convinced that it would be in the interest of the United States to keep Israel out of the picture for as long as possible, it is unlikely that any of its members feared that Israel could not protect itself if Iraq succeeded in overpowering Saudi Arabia. This would have been a worst-case scenario, but one that Israel would been able to cope with quite effectively.

14. Ibid.

15. Ibid.: 253.

16. Scowcroft also attended the meeting.

17. It is very interesting that in his 8 August 1990 television address, President Bush said that he had decided to help Saudi Arabia only after "the Saudi government requested our help." He continued: "And I responded to that request by ordering U.S. air and ground forces to deploy to the Kingdom of Saudi Arabia." He never mentioned that in fact it was he who ordered Secretary Cheney to persuade the Saudi monarch to ask for U.S. assistance.

This was not the first time a president had relied on such a tactic to deploy U.S. military troops. On 23 October 1983, the leaders of Jamaica, Barbados, St. Vincent, St. Lucia, Dominica, St. Kitts-Nevis, Antigua, and Barbuda met with U.S. ambassador Milan Bish and Deputy Assistant Secretary of State for Caribbean Affairs Charles Gillespie to request that the United States organize a joint invasion of Grenada. Such a request, however, was extended only after U.S. officials had made it clear that the Reagan administration would welcome it. Bush, who at that time was serving as vice president, played a key role in the decisio-making process. See Hybel 1990: 271.

18. Quoted in *Defense of Saudi Arabia, Speech of August 8, 1990* (1991): 199. It is critical to keep in mind that, immediately after the speech, President Bush stated that the U.S. forces in Saudi Arabia were in a defensive mode and that it was not their mission to drive the Iraqis out of Kuwait. But in his statement he never suggested that such a defensive mode would not be altered. "Well, as you know from what I said, they're there in a defensive mode now. And therefore, that is not the mission, to drive the Iraqis out of Kuwait. We have economic sanctions that I hope will be effective to the end, and I don't know how long they will be there."

19. Elizabeth Drew arrives at a similar conclusion. She argues that from the very beginning the decision was made hastily without the full airing of opinions. See Drew 1991: 184.

20. Here I take a stand different from that adopted by Elizabeth Drew. She contends that one of the reasons Bush chose to go to war against Saddam is that the former had been "spoiling for a battle with [the Iraqi leader] for sometime." See Drew 1991: 183.

I do not think the evidence backs Drew's argument. Bush had not been "spoiling for a fight" with Saddam for quite some time. On the contrary, the president and his associates had worked hard to find ways to accommodate Iraq's interests without undermining the United States's.

21. It is interesting that Bush and his associates, who because of their educational background would be expected to possess a general understanding of history, never considered the possibility of using Japan's decision to attack Pearl Harbor in 1941 as a useful explanatory case. As Daniel Yergin notes, the "Japanese attacked Pearl Harbor to protect their flanks as they grabbed for the petroleum resources of the East Indies" (Yergin 1991: 24). To Yergin's argument one should add that Japanese leaders were drawn to take this drastic step only after the United States and other Western powers had placed an embargo on the export of oil to Japan. See Hybel 1986: 29–30.

22. The Hitler analogy became quite popular during the months preceding Bush's final decision to attack Iraqi troops in Kuwait.

23. Ibid.: 317.

24. Quoted in Woodward 1991: 277.

25. Powell remained convinced almost until the very end that Saddam was "rational" and would eventually recognize that his only choice was to pull out of Kuwait. Bush, in turn, had great difficulty accepting that Saddam would not realize what he was facing and how costly it would be to him and Iraq to remain in Kuwait. It was not until late in December that Bush began to accept the idea that his perception of Saddam might have been wrong. But by then all he could manage to ask was: "Is he crazy?" See Woodward 1991: 350.

Very few foreign policy makers and analysts seem to realize that they cannot determine whether an international leader is rational without first accounting for the way in which that leader ranks his values. They tend to take for granted that all decision makers across the international arena invariably rank losing a war as the least desirable outcome. History, however, has shown on more than one occasion that other outcomes may be more objectionable. Japan's decision to attack Pearl Harbor is a case in point. See Hybel 1986: 31. I address this issue in some greater detail in the next two paragraphs.

26. See George and Smoke 1974: 221.

27. Elizabeth Drew agrees with this assessment when she contends that from early on, the analytical and decision-making process was confined to a small group, most of whom seemed to know very little about Saddam Hussein and Iraq. Drew 1991: 184.

28. Woodward 1991: 320.

29. See note 9 in this chapter.

30. Woodward 1991: 255.

31. Ibid.: 255 and 260.

32. Ibid.: 331–32. Former president Jimmy Carter advocated using intermediaries to negotiate with Iraq. See Carter 1991: 225–27. Former Secretary of State Henry Kissinger, on the other hand, claimed that the United States might have to resort to force in order to destroy not Iraq's military, but its nuclear and chemical facilities. See Kissinger 1991: 238–42.

33. Elizabeth Drew confirms the view that Secretary of State Baker was uncomfortable with the idea of going to war with Iraq when she contends that he, more than any other member of the Bush administration, believed that it should attempt to work something out with Saddam. See Drew 1991: 186.

34. Woodward 1991: 300.

35. Ibid.: 301

36. Ibid.: 42 and 302.

37. Ibid.

38. Sorensen 1965: 90.

39. George 1980: 90.

40. Janis 1972.

41. Woodward 1991: 302.

42. George 1980: 90. An example of Secretary of State Baker's tendency to give in to Bush's and Scowcroft's view is his decision to accept their demand that he not travel to Baghdad to meet with Saddam Hussein. According to Elizabeth Drew, Scowcroft did not like the idea of Baker traveling to Baghdad and meeting with

Saddam partly because he feared that the secretary of state might be too inclined to negotiate an agreement. Baker ultimately agreed to meet with Iraq's foreign minister in Geneva. By then, however, there was no chance of reaching any negotiated settlement, because Bush had made it very clear that he was not "in a negotiating mood" and that Iraq had to "withdraw without condition." See Drew 1991: 186.

43. Woodward 1991:.225.

44. According to Colin Powell, Bush's behavior during important meetings was very different from Ronald Reagan's. As Woodward explains, Bush "wanted to be the player, the guy who made as many of the calls as possible." Woodward 1991: 225.

45. It is no wonder that Colin Powell came to refer to Bush's closer advisers as the "big guys." Woodward 1991: 302.

46. As an official in the Bush administration put it, sanctions and diplomacy were nothing more than the political precursors of war; each was a "box to check." See Drew 1991: 181.

47. See Klare 1991: 474. His article is a useful analysis of the new U.S. military doctrine designed to respond to an international environment in which the Soviet Union is no longer its second most powerful actor.

48. Ibid.

49. Quoted in Woodward 1991: 324.

50. Bush was obviously referring to the military when he stated: "I know whose backside's at stake and rightfully so." See Woodward 1991: 339.

51. The first set of figures was based on a worst-case planning model presented in Saudi Arabia on 1 December by General Schwarzkopf to Secretary of Defense Cheney and General Powell. The second set, beginning with the number of U.S. planes the military expected to lose, was delivered to President Bush on 1 December by the new Air Force chief, Gen. Merrill McPeak. See Woodward 1991: 349, 340–41.

52. Ibid.: 300.

53. Ibid.: 262.

54. Ibid.: 320

55. The formal authorization was not sent until 29 December, but by then Schwarzkopf and his superiors in Washington had already agreed on a date and time. Ibid.: 352–54.

56. I am using "satisfying" and "maximization" as proposed by Richard Cyert, James March, and Herbert Simon. See March and Simon 1958 and Cyert and March 1963.

Chapter 5

1. See Waltz 1979: 63 and Keohane 1984: 25.

2. Keohane 1984: 25.

3. Ibid. See also Waltz 1979: 71.

4. This seems to be the position adopted by Keohane. See Keohane 1984: 27.

5. Waltz 1979: 8.

6. Ibid.: 121–22.

7. Ibid.: 122.

8. It is important to note that not everybody agrees with the contention that a bipolar system is more stable than a multipolar system. See, for instance, Deutsch and Singer 1964: 390–406.

9. Waltz 1979: 61.

10. I, for one, never make such claim in my book *How Leaders Reason.*

11. Those who contend that capitalism leads to imperialism have, until recently, been unwilling to acknowledge that imperialism may result from factors other than the economic structure of a state.

12. Waltz may wish to contend, for instance, that it was the "tightening of the Soviet Union's control over the states of Eastern Europe [that] led to the Marshall Plan and the Atlantic Defense Treaty," but the relationship between the international structure and the policy was not as deterministic as he assumes it was. He

cannot guarantee that a different administration with a different set of values and goals would have responded as the Truman administration did. Can he claim that had Franklin Roosevelt been alive his administration would have not chosen a different path? See Waltz 1979: 171.

13. Foreign policies and international structures are interconnected in two different ways. During the making of the foreign policy, what counts is the decision maker's perception of the international structure; during the implementation of the foreign policy, as the emphasis switches to the analysis of its effects, what is important is whether the foreign policy maker's definition of the international structure corresponds with the structure's "objective reality." See Sprout and Sprout 1957: 309–328.

14. See Krasner 1978: 40–41.

15. Robert Keohane notes that my view of "explanation" is Aristotelian, and would not be accepted as a theoretical explanation by post-Galileans. As he argues, to observe the actions of a decision maker and then match them to one of the cognitive patterns identified—e.g., to attribution theory, cognitive consistency theory, or schema theory—does not constitute a theoretical explanation. The most it can be called, he adds, is a systematic description.

Keohane is right, but his argument must be qualified. There is no question that this study can only claim to postulate a systematic description of Bush's decision-making process. Other analysts, however, can rely on this analysis to formulate two different types of explanations. First, they can use this study to explain and predict how George Bush would respond to similar international problems in the future. Needless to say, the chances of a similar occurrence crossing Bush's path is most unlikely. This leaves us with the second type of explanation.

In the United States, political candidates for the presidency are asked to reveal their political, economic, and social plans, among other things. In addition, they are expected to demonstrate that they possess leadership qualities. Neither the public nor the media, however, has ever sought to really understand how political candidates reason or how they look at problems and attempt to resolve them. Deep knowledge of how they reason can help voters gauge whether candidates can be trusted to deal effectively with complex issues, and help students of U.S. foreign policy to explain and predict how they would address international problems.

Notwithstanding this qualification, I am grateful to Robert Keohane for his insightful comments and suggestions.

16. I am particularly grateful to one of the anonymous readers for pointing out in her/his critique of an earlier draft that my empirical argument seemed to indicate that there was a connection between cognitive consistency and schema theory but that I never acknowledged their relationship in my conclusion.

17. See Lebow 1981: 102–5; and Jervis 1976: 224.

18. See Janis and Mann 1977: 13.

19. By "open" I mean that they openly verbalize their differences inside the immediate circuit of decision makers, including the president.

20. See Burke and Greenstein 1991: 11 and 14.

21. Orwell 1957: 157. Reason and rationality are not synonyms, but rationality without reason is not possible.

22. For an insightful comparison between Greek democracy and contemporary democracy, see Sartori 1987: vol. 2, chap. 10. See also Dahl 1989: chaps. 1 and 2.

23. I am using the term "masses" as a sociological concept, similar to that postulated by Ortega y Gasset. See Ortega y Gasset, 1957: 13–14.

24. See Macpherson 1973: 5.

25. By "liberal democracy" I mean a democracy with a capitalist economic foundation.

26. Chile and Uruguay are the two democracies that gave way to military regimes during the 1970s and 1980s, but now seem to be back on track; France was one of the states that had to alter its overall political structure during the 1950s by extending greater decision making powers to its executive.

27. De Tocqueville 1945: vol. 1, 243.

28. Ibid.

29. Alexis de Tocqueville suggested something similar when he stated: "In foreign policies it is rare for the interest of the aristocracy to be distinct from that of the people" (de Tocqueville,

1945: vol. 1, 244). With the dramatic change in the conditions under which international interactions take place, this argument has been widely challenged, particularly by Marxist and dependency theorists. See Wallerstein 1974; Frank 1969; and Cardoso and Faletto 1979.

30. For an extensive discussion of the dilemma faced by democracies as they seek to balance the costs of not having full representation and the costs of formulating a policy with full representation, see Buchanan and Tullock 1974.

31. See Gilpin 1983: 232.

32. In fairness to Gilpin, his argument is significantly less deterministic. Ibid.: 231–44.

33. Ibid.: 232.

34. Robert Keohane and Joseph Nye differentiate between "sensitivity" and "vulnerability." By sensitivity they mean "liability to costly effects imposed from outside before policies are altered to try to change the situation." By vulnerability they mean "an actor's liability to suffer costs imposed by external events even after policies have been altered." See Keohane and Nye 1977: 13.

35. Williamson 1963: 238.

36. A different, but related, argument is suggested by Robert Keohane when he proposes that small "states do not have the luxury of deciding whether or how fast to adjust to external change. They do not seek change; it is thrust upon them. Powerful countries can postpone adjustment." See Keohane 1984: 179.

I am somewhat uncomfortable with Keohane's distinction. Although it is correct to assume that all weak states are vulnerable, I do not think it is appropriate to suggest that powerful states are never vulnerable. Thus, rather than differentiating between weak and powerful states, I think it is preferable to separate them in terms of their respective levels of vulnerability.

Notwithstanding my qualification, I am grateful to Robert Keohane for suggesting that I relate my original argument to the economic argument and for reminding me of his own thesis in *After Hegemony* (1984).

37. I purposely qualified the proposition. "By some vulnerable states" I mean very weak states. Weak states seldom have the

resources and technology necessary to engage in rational analyses. I will identify a second paradox below.

38. See Jervis 1976; Holsti 1972; Janis 1972; Hermann 1969; and Paige 1968.

39. This argument is not that different from Kenneth Waltz's contention that the structure of an international system affects behavior within the system through the socialization of the actors. See Waltz 1979: 74–75.

40. Ibid.: 232.

41. According to Robert Keohane and Joseph Nye, the "vulnerability dimension of interdependence rests on the relative availability and costliness of the alternatives that various actors face." See Keohane and Nye 1977: 13. From this definition it can be inferred that the greater an actor's relative power vis-a-vis other international actors, the greater the availability of alternatives and the lower their costs.

42. It is critical to keep in mind that I am not contending that the foreign policy makers in Washington will automatically become more rational with an increase in the vulnerability of the United States. I still hold that the ability of foreign policy makers to be rational is ultimately a function of their own internal characteristics. My argument is simply that if we were to hold constant the personalities of the decision makers, such individuals are more likely to be rational when they experience some degree of vulnerability.

43. Quoted in Gaddis 1982: 279.

44. A major exception to this rule was the Carter administration. For a discussion of Jimmy Carter's perception of the national interest of the United States and of its role in the international arena, see Hybel 1990: 283–88.

45. The event that I am referring to is the invasion of Panama by U.S. forces in December 1989. It is helpful to keep in mind that George Bush could have moved against Manuel Noriega a few months earlier, but refrained. This decision was widely criticized in the United States and may have convinced President Bush that a properly organized invasion would not be a particularly risky undertaking and would enhance his image at home, as Ronald

Reagan's image was enhanced in 1983.

46. It is no wonder that Saddam Hussein was one of the few international leaders to speak positively about the coup against Mikhail Gorbachev in August 1991. He is reported to have stated that the reestablishment of a conservative regime in the Soviet Union would bring back to the Middle East the proper balance. See the *New York Times*, 21 August 1991.

47. It remains a question whether Saddam, knowing full well that the Soviet Union was no longer an effective counterbalance in the Middle East and suspicious that Washington would exploit the imbalance, accounted for both factors as he tried to figure out how to respond to Bush's demand that Iraq pull out of Kuwait.

48. This is the principal problem with Morgenthau's Realist theory. His commitment to rationality leads him to assume that foreign policy makers can be perceived as "rational actors." Time and again Morgenthau recognizes that decision makers are not rational, and argues that in order for the United States to be effective in international affairs its leaders must act rationally. But failure by decision makers to act rationally undermines the explanatory and predictive value of his theory.

49. Or as Louis Halle put it: "In the degree that the image is false, no technicians, however efficient, can make the policy that is based on it sound." See Halle 1960: 318.

50. See George 1980: 56–57.

51. See Carbonell 1983: 151–52; and Hybel 1990: 28.

52. Oppenheimer 1956: 127–35.

53. Jervis 1976: 220.

54. See George 1980: 58–60.

55. See Heradstveit 1979.

56. See Sartori 1987: vol. 2, 430–31.

57. I do not mean to suggest that a politician who is good at playing the domestic political game will be equally successful at playing the international political game. President Lyndon Johnson's domestic political skills rarely served him well when he had to address international problems. And vice versa, George Bush, whom

many perceived as a capable international player, was quite ineffective when dealing with domestic political issues. I am merely suggesting that in order to address either domestic or international issues, leaders must possess a minimum set of political skills.

58. By "technical issues," I mean not only issues that are scientifically related, but also issues that demand an understanding of economics and the political, social, and cultural nature of other states.

Bibliography

Abelson, Robert. 1976. "Script Processing in Attitude Formation and Decision-making." In *Cognition and Social Behavior*, edited by J. S. Carroll and J. W. Payne. Hillsdale, N.J.: Lawrence Erlbaum Associates.

Achen, Christopher, and Duncan Snidal 1989. "Rational Deterrence Theory and Comparative Case Studies," *World Politics* 41, no.2 (January): 143–69.

Allison, Graham. 1971. *Essence of Decision: Explaining the Cuban Missile Crisis*. Boston: Little, Brown.

Ambrose, Stephen. 1984. *Eisenhower: The President*, Vol. II. New York: Simon and Schuster.

Axelrod, Robert, ed. 1976. *Structure of Decision*. Princeton: Princeton University Press.

Bentham, Jeremy. 1834. *Deontology*. London: Longman.

Berman, Larry. 1982. *Planning a Tragedy: The Americanization of the War in Vietnam*. New York: W.W. Norton and Company.

Brzezinski, Zbigniew. 1983. *Power and Principle: Memoirs of the National Security Advisor, 1977–1981*. New York: Farrar, Straus, Giroux.

Buchanan, James M., and Gordon Tullock. 1974. *The Calculus of Consent*. Ann Arbor: The University of Michigan Press.

Bull, Hedley. 1977. *The Anarchical Society*. New York: Columbia University Press.

Bulloch, John, and Harvey Morris. 1991. *Saddam's War: The Origins of the Kuwait Conflict and the International Response*. London: Faber and Faber.

Bulloch, John, and Harvey Morris. 1989. *The Gulf War: Its Origins, History and Consequences*. London: Methuen.

Burke, John, and Fred I. Greenstein. 1989. *How Presidents Test Reality: Decisions on Vietnam, 1954 and 1965*. New York: Russell Sage Foundation.

Bush, George. 1991. "Defense of Saudi Arabia Speech of August 8, 1990." In *The Gulf War Reader, History, Documents, Opinions*, edited by Micah L. Sifry and Christopher Cerf. New York: Random House.

Cannon, Lou. 1991. *President Reagan. The Role of a Lifetime*. New York: Simon and Schuster.

Carbonnell, Jaime G. 1983. "Learning by Analogy: Formulation and Generalizing Plans from Past Experience." In *Machine Learning in Artificial Intelligence Approach*, edited by Ryszarol S. Michalski, Jaime G. Carbonell, and Tom M. Mitchells. Palo Alto, CA: Tioga Publishing Company.

Cardoso, Fernando Henrique, and Enzo Faletto. 1979. *Dependency and Development in Latin America*. Berkeley: University of California Press.

Carter, Jimmy. 1991. "The Need to Negotiate." In *The Gulf War Reader*, edited by Sifry and Cerf.

Clausewitz, Karl von. 1990. "On the Nature of War." In *Classics of International Relations*, edited by John A. Vasquez. Englewood Cliffs, N.J.: Prentice-Hall.

Cyert, Richard M., and James G. March. 1963. *A Behavioral Theory of the Firm*. Englewood Cliffs, N.J.: Prentice-Hall, Inc.

Dahl, Robert A. 1989. *Democracy and its Critics*. New Haven: Yale University Press.

Davidson, D. L. 1916. *Political Thought in England. The Utilitarians from Bentham to J. T. Mill*. New York: Holt, Reinhart, and Winston, Inc.

Deutsch, Karl W., and J. David Singer. 1964. "Multipolar Power Systems and International Stability." *World Politics* 16, (April).

Draper, Theodore. 1991. "American Hubris." In *The Gulf War Reader*, edited by Sifry and Cerf.

Drew, Elizabeth. 1991. "Washington Prepares for War." In *The Gulf War Reader*, edited by Sifry and Cerf.

Economist, The. 1991. "Kuwait: How the West Blundered." In *The Gulf Reader*, edited by Sifry and Cerf.

Frank, Andre Gunder. 1969. *Capitalism and Underdevelopment in Latin America*. New York: Modern Reader Paperbacks.

Gaddis, John Lewis. 1982. *Strategies of Containment*. Oxford: Oxford University Press.

Garst, Daniel. 1989. "Thucydides and Neorealism." *International Studies Quarterly* 33, 1.

George, Alexander L. 1980. *Presidential Decisionmaking in Foreign Policy: The Effective Use of Information and Advice*. Boulder, Colo.: Westview Press.

George, Alexander L., and Richard Smoke. 1974. *Deterrence and American Foreign Policy*. New York: Columbia University Press.

George, Alexander L. 1969. "The 'Operational Code': A Neglected Approach to the Study of Political Leaders and Decision-Making." *International Studies Quarterly* (June).

Gilpin, Robert. 1984. "The Richness of the Tradition of Political Realism." *International Organization* 38.

Glaspie Transcript, The. 1991. "Saddam Meets the U.S. Ambassador (July 25, 1991)." *In The Gulf Reader*, edited by Sifry and Cerf.

Gomme, A. W. 1962. "Four Passages in Thucydides." In *More Essays on Greek History and Culture*, edited by D. A. Campbell. Oxford: Basil Blackwell.

Greenstein, Fred. 1982. *The Hidden-Hand Presidency*. New York: Basic Books.

Haig, Alexander. 1983. *Caveat*. New York: Macmillan.

Halle, Louis. 1960. *American Foreign Policy*. London: G. Allen.

Heradstveit, Daniel. 1970. *The Arab-Israeli Conflict: Psychological Obstacles to Peace*. Oslo: Universitetsforlaget.

Hermann, Charles. 1969. *A Simulation Analysis*. Indianapolis, Ind.: Bobbs-Merrill.

Holsti, Ole. 1976. "Foreign Policy Formation Viewed Cognitively." In *Structure of Decision*, edited by Robert Axelrod.

Holsti, Ole. 1972. *Crisis, Escalation, War*. Montreal: McGill-Queen's University Press.

Hybel, Alex Roberto. 1990. *How Leaders Reason: US Intervention in the Caribbean Basin and Latin America*. Oxford: Basil Blackwell.

Hybel, Alex Roberto. 1986. *The Logic of Surprise in International Conflict*. Lexington, Mass.: Lexington Books.

Janis, Irving L., and Leon Mann. 1977. *Decisionmaking: Psychological Analyses of Conflict, Choice, and Commitment*. New York: Free Press.

Janis, Irving L. 1972. *Victims of Groupthink*. Boston: Houghton Mifflin.

Jervis, Robert. 1976. *Perception and Misperception in International Politics*. Princeton: Princeton University Press.

Kelley, Harold H. 1967. "Attribution Theory in Social Psychology." In *Nebraska Symposium on Motivation*. Lincoln: University of Nebraska Press.

Keohane, Robert O. 1984. *After Hegemony: Cooperation and Discord in the World Political Economy*. Princeton: Princeton University Press.

Keohane, Robert O. 1983. "Theory of World Politics: Structural Realism and Beyond." In *Political Science: The State of the Discipline*, edited by Ada W. Finifter. Washington, D.C.: The American Political Science Association.

Keohane, Robert O., and Joseph S. Nye. 1977. *Power and Interdependence*. Boston: Little, Brown.

Khadduri, Majid. 1988. *The Gulf War: The Origins and Implications of the Iraq-Iran Conflict*. New York: Oxford University Press.

Khalidi, Walid. 1991. "Iraq vs. Kuwait: Claims and Counterclaims." In *The Gulf War Reader*, edited by Sifry and Cerf.

Kissinger, Henry. 1991. "How to Cut Iraq Down to Size (Testimony Before the Senate Armed Services Committee, November 28, 1990)." In *The Gulf War Reader*, edited by Sifry and Cerf.

Klare, Michael T. 1991. "The Pentagon's New Paradigm." In *The Gulf War Reader*, edited by Sifry and Cerf.

Knorr, Klaus. 1964. "Failures in National Intelligence Estimates: The Case of the Cuban Missiles." *World Politics* 16, no. 1 (April).

Krasner, Stephen D., ed. 1983. *International Regimes*. Ithaca: Cornell University Press.

Krasner, Stephen D. 1978. *Defending the National Interest*. Princeton: Princeton University Press.

Kuhn, Thomas S. 1970. *The Structure of Scientific Revolutions*. Chicago: The University of Chicago Press.

Langer, William, and S. Everett Cleason. 1953. *The Undeclared War*. New York: Harper and Brothers Publishers.

Larson, Deborah. 1985. *Origins of Containment*. Princeton: Princeton University Press.

Lave, Charles A., and James G. March. 1975. *An Introduction to Models in the Social Sciences*. New York: Harper and Row Publishers.

Lebow, Richard Ned. 1981. *Between Peace and War*. Baltimore: The Johns Hopkins University Press.

Lowenthal, Abraham F. 1972. *The Dominican Intervention*. Cambridge: Harvard University Press.

Macpherson, C. B. 1973. *Democratic Theory*. Oxford: Clarendon Press.

March, James G., and Herbert A. Simon. 1958. *Organizations*. New York: Wiley and Sons.

Martin, David C., and John Walcott. 1988. *Best Laid Plans: The Inside Story of America's War Against Terrorism*. New York: Touchstone Books.

Marx, Karl, and Friedrich Engels. 1968. *The Communist Manifesto*. New York: Modern Reader.

Mefford, Dwain. 1985. "Combining Historical Narrative and Game Theory in a Rule Based System." Paper delivered at the Annual Meeting of the Western International Studies Association, Los Angeles, California.

Mesquita, Bueno de. 1981. *The War Trap*. New Haven: Yale University Press.

Morgenthau, Hans. 1985. *Politics Among Nations: The Struggle for Power and Peace*. Revised by Kenneth W. Thompson. New York: Alfred A. Knopf.

Neustadt, Richard E., and Ernest R. May. 1986. *Thinking in Time: The Uses of History for Decision Makers*. New York: The Free Press.

Newsweek, 20 January 1992.

New York Times, 24 June 1992.

New York Times, 21 August 1991.

Nisbett, Richard E., Eugene Borgida, Rick Crandall, and Harvey Reed. 1976. "Popular Induction: Information is Not Always Information." In *Cognition and Social Behavior*, edited by Carroll and Payne. Hillsdale, N.J.: Lawrence Erlbaum Associates.

Nisbett, Richard E., and Lee Ross. 1980. *Human Inference: Strategies and Shortcomings of Social Judgment*. Englewood Cliffs, N.J.: Prentice-Hall.

Ortega y Gasset, Jose. 1957. *The Revolt of the Masses*. New York: W.W. Norton and Company.

Orwell, George. 1957. "Politics and the English Language." In *George Orwell: Selected Essays*. Harmondsworth: Penguin.

Paige, Glenn D. 1968. *The Korean Decision*. New York: The Free Press.

Reagan, Ronald. 1990. *An American Life*. New York: Simon and Schuster.

Report of the President's Special Review Board. 1987. (The Tower Report.)

Ross, Lee. 1977. "The Intuitive Psychologist and his Shortcomings: Distortions and the Attribution Process." In *Experimental Social Psychology*, 10, edited by Leonard Berkowitz, 174–220. New York: Academic Press.

Sartori, Giovanni. 1987. *The Theory of Democracy Revisited*. Vol. 2. Chatham, N.J.: Chatham House Publishers, Inc.

Sartori, Giovanni. 1975. "The Tower of Babel." In Giovanni Sartori, Fred W. Riggs, and Henry Teune, *Tower of Babel: On the Definition and Analysis of Concepts in the Social Sciences.* Occasional Paper No. 6. Pittsburgh, Pa.: International Studies Association.

Seaton, Albert. 1971. *The Russo-German War, 1941–1945.* London: Arthur Baker.

Schrodt, Philip A. 1986. "Pattern Matching, Set Prediction and Foreign Policy Analysis." In *Artificial Intelligence and Foreign Policy,* edited by Stephen Cimbala. Lexington, Mass.: Lexington Books.

Sick, Gary. 1989. "The United States and the Persian Gulf." In *The Gulf War: Regional and International Dimensions,* edited by Hanns W. Maull and Otto Pick. New York: St. Martin's Press.

Simon, Herbert. 1957. *Models of Man.* New York: John Wiley and Sons.

Sorensen, Theodore. 1963. *Decision-making in the White House.* New York: Columbia University Press.

Sprout, Harold, and Margaret Sprout. 1957. "Environmental Factors in the Study of International Politics." *Journal of Conflict Resolution* 1.

Stein, Janice Gross. 1982. "Military Deception, Strategic Surprise, and Conventional Deterrence: A Political Analysis of Egypt and Israel, 1971–1973." *Journal of Strategic Studies* 5, no. 1 (March).

Steinbruner, John D. 1974. *The Cybernetic Theory of Decision.* Princeton: Princeton University Press.

Stork Joe, and Martha Wenger. 1991. "From Rapid Deployment to Massive Deployment." In *The Gulf War Reader,* edited by Sifry and Cerf.

Thucydides. 1982. *The Peloponnesian War.* New York: The Modern Library.

Tocqueville, Alexis de. 1945. *Democracy in America.* Vol. 2. New York: Vintage Books.

Tucker, Robert C. ed. 1972. *The Marx-Engels Reader.* New York: W.W. Norton.

Walker, Stephen G. 1977. "The Interface Between Beliefs and Behavior: Henry Kissinger's Operational Code and the Vietnam War." *Journal of Conflict Resolution* (March).

Vandenbroucke, Lucien. 1984. "Anatomy of a Failure: The Decision to Land at the Bay of Pigs." *Political Science Quarterly,* 99, no. 3 (Fall): 471–91.

Wallerstein, Immanuel. 1974. *The Modern World System.* New York: Academic Press.

Waltz, Kenneth N. 1979. *Theory of International Politics.* New York: Random House.

Weinberger, Caspar. 1990. *Fighting for Peace: Seven Critical Years in the Pentagon.* New York: Warner Books.

Whaley, Barton. 1973. *Codeword Barbarossa.* Cambridge: The MIT Press.

Williamson, Oliver E. 1963. "A Model of Rational Managerial Behavior." In *A Behavioral Theory of the Firm,* by Richard Cliffs and James G. March. Englewood Cliffs, N.J.: Prentice-Hall Inc.

Woodward, Bob. 1991. *The Commanders.* New York: Simon and Schuster.

Yergin, Daniel. 1991. "Oil: The Strategic Prize." In *The Gulf War Reader,* edited by Sifry and Cerf.

Zagare, Frank C. 1990. "Rationality and Deterrence." *World Politics* 42, no. 2 (January): 238–60.

Index

Abelson, Robert, 21, 109
Achen, Christopher, 17; on rationality, 17–19, 104, 106, 107
Allison, Graham, 17, 103
Arab League, 36
Assad, (President of Syria) Hafez, 43
attribution theory, 1, 5, 19–23, 25, 100, 106; and President Bush, 65, 79, 87; and rationality, 6, 20, 23, 86
Axelrod, Robert, 3, 16, 104

Baker III, (Secretary of State) James, 39–40, 50; and decision to use military force to expel Iraq from Kuwait, 72; and foreign policy making process, 78, 121; and sanctions against Iraq, 70, 72
Brzezinski, (National Security Advisor) Zbigniew, 41, 42, 114
Bush administration. See Bush, (President) George
Bush, (President) George, 7, 27, 35, 50, 128; and covert action against Saddam

Hussein, 62; and decision to protect Saudi Arabia, 8–9, 60, 61, 62, 64, 65, 67, 119; and decision to use military force to expel Iraq from Kuwait, 8–9, 69–70, 73, 79, 119; and foreign policy making process, 74–75, 77; and Hitler analogy, 9, 68, 120; and Kuwait, 9, 33, 70; and Munich analogy, 8–9, 66, 75, 76, 79; and policy of deterrence, 7; and rationality, 8, 10, 87; and relation with Iraq prior to August 1990, 51–53, 116; and sanctions against Iraq, 70, 72, 73, 75; and surprise, 55, 65; and U.S. vulnerability, 96–97; and Vietnam syndrome, 9, 76, 77, 79; on Cheney's visit to King Fahd, 64; on Saddam Hussein, 9, 50–53, 65–66, 67–69, 75, 79, 112, 120; on sale of weapons to Iran, 48; on whether to protect Saudi Arabia or free Kuwait, 63
Butler, (Lt. Gen., Head of Plans and Policy at Pentagon) George Lee, 71; on containment, 71

Hussein, (President of Iraq)
Saddam, 7, 29, 30, 31, 32,
33, 40, 48, 51, 52, 53; and
April Glaspie, 31, 37–40;
and Bush Administration, 7;
and Hitler, 35, 113; and
Iran, 112; and Israel, 35–36;
and King Hussein, 34, 97;
and Kuwait, 7, 36, 37, 38,
111; and President Hosni
Mubarak, 34, 97; and
surprise, 33, 34, 54, 116;
and Soviet Union, 34, 128;
and United States, 34; on
overproduction of oil by
Kuwait, 30, 37, 112
Hybel, Alex Roberto, 4, 109,
110, 111, 112, 113, 123, 127

Jervis, Robert, 3, 16, 104, 109,
116, 127, 128
Johnson administartion, 3
Jones, (Gen., Chairman Joint
Chiefs of Staff) David C.,
71; on sanctions against
Iraq, 71

Kelley, Harold, 20, 108, 109
Kelley, (Lt. Gen., Director of
Operations at the Pentagon)
Thomas, 30; on Iraq's plan
to attack Kuwait, 30–31.
Kemp, (Middle East Expert,
National Security Council)
Geoffrey, 45
Kennedy administration, 3,
25; and cognitive
consistency theory, 110, 111
Keohane, Robert, 15, 105, 106,
123; on Aristotelian versus

post-Galilean approach to
theory building, 124–25; on
cooperation, 15; on egoist
rational actors, 15; on
regimes, 15; on
vulnerability, 126, 127
Kissinger, (National Security
Advisor and Secretary of
State) Henry, 96–97, 121

Lang, (Pentagon analyst for
the Middle East and South
Asia region) Walter, 29; on
Iraq'a plan to attack Kuwait,
29–33, 36, 41, 113; on Saddam
Hussein, 31–32, 36, 64
Larson, Deborah, 4, 105, 106,
108; on cognitive
approaches, 16

McFarland, (National Security
Advisor) Robert, 46; on sale
of weapons to Iran, 47–48;
on war in Lebanon, 46
Morgenthau, Hans, 2, 104,
105; and national interest,
2; and power, 2; and
rationality, 2, 3, 128
Mubarak, (President of Egypt)
Hosni, 34, 97
Muskie (Secretary of State)
Edmund, 42

Nisbett, Richard, 108, 109

Powell, (Gen., Chairman Joint
Chiefs of Staff) Colin, 7, 39,
40, 41, 45, 49, 50, 60; and
decision to protect Saudi